M000098475

a MJN Publishing book

International Student Pathfinder:

The Essential Guide
on UK Universities
and Careers

From the reviews of
International Student Pathfinder:

"Essential reading for all international applicants to the UK universities."
- Brian Heap, Author of HEAP 2019: University Degree Course Offers

"A well-written and highly informative guide that should be on any prospective student's reading list, whether or not they are planning to study overseas. There is so much within the covers of this book that I wish I had been privy to when I was considering a course of study and my choice of colleges. The author sets out simple strategies designed to help students turn their career aspirations into real job offers. Those who hadn't considered overseas study may well end up doing so after reading the author's work as well as the student testimonials he provides throughout the book. *International Student Pathfinder* is most highly recommended."
– Jack Magnus for Readers' Favourite

"The author has written a must-read guide for the overseas student. Wrong decisions can be expensive both in cost and time. You need to make a rational, informed decision on university choice and thereafter to ensure your time at university is productive and enjoyable. This book constructively covers key issues that will support you into the right university, your stay there and your career choices on completion of your degree."
- Emeritus Professor Philip Thomas, Former Director of International Recruitment, Cardiff University

"Marvin Nyenyezi writes with simplicity and offers real-life examples while weaving interesting stories into the book. This is a guide for international students on the UK that helps them to understand their new world, make intelligent decisions, and gather the tools they need for a successful academic journey. It is packed with wisdom and insight and reflects the world international students need to know."
- Romuald Dzemo for Readers' Favorite

Author: Marvin Nyenyezi

This is a MJN Publishing book.

MJN Publishing, Worcester, England, UK.

Copyright © MJN Publishing 2019.

British Library Cataloguing in Publication Data

A catalogue record for this book is available from the British Library

ISBN: 978-1-5272-3477-2

Cover design: Vanessa Mendozzi

Internal layout: Luca Funari

International Student Pathfinder:

The Essential Guide
on UK Universities
and Careers

Marvin Nyenyezi

Contents

Acknowledgments 13

About the author 15

About this book 17

Why write a book for international students? 17

What the book covers 19

How the book is structured 20

Introduction 23

The attraction of UK universities 23

Intense competition for graduate jobs 27

PART ONE: Before university 31

CHAPTER 1: Choosing your university - it is important

where you study 33

Understanding the university system 35

Why the university you attend matters 43

Reputation 44

Rankings and league tables 46

Teaching excellence and student outcomes 49

Employment prospects 54

CHAPTER 2: How to assess universities on employability and entrepreneurship **67**

The Alumni network 67

Campus visits 68

Online research 69

Graduate success story: Jianqiao (China) 84

CHAPTER 3: Choosing the right course - it matters what subject you study **87**

Short term: how subjects, jobs and salaries compare 90

Long term: how subjects, jobs and salaries compare 109

Graduate success story: Edward (Ghana) 123

PART TWO: While at university **127**

CHAPTER 4: First year **129**

New beginnings 129

Culture shock 130

Laying the foundations for career development 136

Entrepreneurship success story:
Launching a ride-sharing company in India 147

CHAPTER 5: Penultimate year **157**

Actions to advance your career development 159

Postgraduate study 163

Managing your busy schedule 166

Graduate success story: Ronald (Uganda) 169

CHAPTER 6: The recruitment process **173**

Application forms and CVs 175

Interviews...182

Assessment centres..192

CHAPTER 7: Final year...**197**

Early deadlines on graduate schemes.................................198

Pursuing work experience...201

Appointments with the Careers Service..............................201

Personal tutors...202

Entrepreneurship opportunities...202

Finish strong..203

Graduate success story: Ajay (India)..................................206

**PART THREE: Graduation and transitioning into
your career**...**209**

CHAPTER 8: Celebrate your success..................**211**

CHAPTER 9: Resilience for the post-graduation slump...............**213**

Entrepreneurship success story:
Building a software business in the UK...............................223

CHAPTER 10: Last thoughts.................................**227**

Appendices..**229**

Appendix 1: Additional sources of information on university
related topics...229

Appendix 2: The Times Top 100 Graduate Employers.....................231

Bibliography...**233**

Endnotes...**235**

Acknowledgments

I would like to thank all my friends and family who have supported me in writing this book. I am so grateful for their unwavering support and encouragement.

I would like to thank Brian Heap for his encouragement and advice. I am also grateful for all the varied contributions from the community of former students who were willing to share their stories for the benefit of future students. Particular thanks are due to: Ronald, Edward, Jianqiao, Ajay, Raghav, Vinay, Alok, Niroshan, Angela, Julie, Alex, Nkatha, Omer, Diane and Krystal.

Lastly, I would like to thank my parents and my dear wife, without whom none of my success would have been possible. To them this book is dedicated.

About the author

Marvin Nyenyezi is a banking professional with over ten years' experience in the UK financial services industry, including retail and commercial banking and insurance and investment markets. His experience includes both in-house advisory roles at leading global organisations such as HSBC and Zurich Insurance and consulting roles at Deloitte.

He obtained his undergraduate degree in Law, LLB (Hons) from Cardiff University. He then attained a Master in Banking and Finance Law (LLM) from King's College London and a Master in Business Administration (MBA) from Cranfield School of Management.

His passion for helping students began during his postgraduate studies where he helped his peers from various overseas backgrounds to get into graduate roles at top global companies. Throughout his career, he has been actively involved with graduate recruitment and delivered careers advice workshops at universities and schools. He is actively involved in supporting charitable initiatives, such as the Prince's Trust, which are aimed at helping young people develop their career skills.

He lives in England with his wife, Chantal, and they have two children, Ariella and Caileb. He is active in his community church where he serves as an Elder on the leadership team and heads up a team of volunteers.

About this book

Why write a book for international students?

The simple answer is because of the lack of guidance tailored towards the needs of thousands of overseas students who come to the UK every year. Whilst many books are aimed at students and graduates, they do not cater to the specific needs of international students and the unique challenges they will encounter.

Most students are sold on the dream of overseas study in the UK expecting to land a rewarding career by the time they graduate. For some, that dream turns into reality as they secure graduate careers with top global companies after graduation. For many, the harsh reality that overseas study alone is not a "golden ticket" to a rewarding career often dawns after they have already forked out thousands of pounds in tuition and living expenses (estimated to be around £22,000 per year)[1].

I was one of those who took the leap and invested in higher education in the UK. My undergraduate and post-graduate experience has provided first-hand insight into the encounters international students face as they try to launch their graduate careers. Although I managed to secure a graduate career, it was an arduous journey. That journey, however, has proved useful in developing a sound understanding about successful strategies that students can adopt to increase their chances of securing graduate jobs.

There is insufficient guidance to help students navigate all the career-impacting choices they must make on their journeys from high school to university graduation. Most books do not make the connection between the choices students make before, during and after university to their career prospects after they graduate. By the time students and graduates realise that they need to take action and work towards enhancing their career prospects, it is too late, and they have lost the advantage.

Many graduates find themselves regretting that they could have done things differently or wishing they had started their career planning much earlier. Plotted along the timeline from before university choices are made right up to graduation, the *International Student Pathfinder* ("*Pathfinder*") will show students what they really need to know and what they need to do. It is an essential guide for students, helping them to navigate all the twists and meandering of their career paths.

Most books on the subject do not fully reflect the experience of students and graduates. *Pathfinder* provides real-life perspectives of graduates. I have interacted with many students, graduate recruiters, careers advisers and gained invaluable insights which are covered in this book. I have experienced both sides of recruitment; as an applicant for graduate roles and as a hiring manager. It is this wealth of experience that I have tried to convey in this book.

Every strategy I share in this book is based on my experience and that of many other graduates. Although there is no secret formula or magical solution, it will guide students and graduates through the labyrinth of choices they have to make and equip them with the tools and strategies they need to succeed.

This book contains insights from former students from many different countries, including India, China, Ghana, Kenya and Uganda. These graduates have developed successful careers in the UK and abroad. Some have established their careers at leading global companies like Amazon, Deloitte and HSBC. Others have gone on to public sector careers or launched their own businesses.

If applied carefully, the insights gained from this book will give students a head-start on the competition and help them devise a successful career plan. Readers will benefit from insight on how to choose your university to making successful graduate applications, performance at assessment centres, interviews and many other important topics.

Going to university is still one of the best career strategies, but only if you seize every opportunity you can find to boost your career prospects. Reading this book will show you how to do it.

What the book covers

Students go to university for a variety of reasons, such as achieving academic qualifications or developing the skills and knowledge that will prepare them for future careers. The university experience is often viewed as a rite of passage – the prelude (albeit an expensive one) to an independent adult life. Therefore, university is appealing because of the fun social life and the opportunity to establish lifelong friendships and live away from home.

For international students, the reasons for choosing to study at a UK university include: attaining academic qualifications from famous institutions, experiencing a different culture, meeting new friends and colleagues from different countries, and many others.

There's no doubt that the university experience has much to offer. However, I believe the main goal for going to university is to achieve a qualification that will help you get into a good career. After all, it will be a significant investment of your money and time, and you want something to show for it at the end aside from massive debts. As such, this book is focused on helping you to achieve your career goals.

Given the increasing interest in entrepreneurship amongst the millennial generation, I have devoted significant consideration to entrepreneurship as a desired graduate outcome. Budding entrepreneurs will find this information useful in planning and preparing for careers as founders of start-up ventures.

Even though you may have no plans of starting your own business, you may be interested in developing entrepreneurship skills and attributes to prepare you to become an "intrapreneur" with an established organisation.

There is a lot of information you may wish to consider to make the most of university. For instance, you may want to know about life in the UK, entrance requirements, fees and funding options, availability of accommodation, immigration rules, etc. These topics are not covered in this book. However, you can find recommendations for additional sources of information on university-related topics in Appendix 1.

How the book is structured

This book is structured along the timeline of the student journey from the pre-university stage right up to the time they graduate. This chronological approach helps students to start planning from an early stage so that they can make the right choices at all the key phases of their career journeys.

A recurring theme from many students is that they wish they had received guidance earlier in their careers – even before they had made their university applications.

This is certainly a view that I share, and it reflects in how this book has been written.

Typically, most books view graduate recruitment and the university experience as separate processes. In fact, a study by the *UK Higher Education International Unit* notes that university departments have operated independently for many years and fall short on making the connection between student experience and graduate outcomes.[2] In reality, the two are inextricably linked.

Your chances for a successful career will be greatly enhanced if your career strategies are linked with your university experience.

You can use this book sequentially or read the chapters in any order you want. Regardless of the stage you're at in your journey, *Pathfinder* can be your essential handbook, helping you to gain the advantage and putting your career objectives on a sure footing.

Introduction

The attraction of UK universities

The international student market is expected to grow significantly. Estimated projections from UNESCO are that overseas student numbers will grow from 4.5 million globally in 2012 to 7 million by 2025.[3] In 2016-17, there were approximately 442,375 overseas students studying at UK universities, representing 19% of all UK higher education enrolment.[4]

The UK is the second most popular destination in the world for international students. In fact, universities are one of the most successful British exports, with international students generating about £7.3 billion annually to the UK economy.[5]

Over the last few years, there has been a trend towards UK universities setting up campuses abroad. There are now almost 40 foreign campuses of British universities in countries like Malaysia, Mauritius, UAE, and Bangladesh. The appeal of these foreign campuses is that students want to gain a high quality education but at a cheaper cost, as they can avoid all the expenses of living in the UK. Additionally, studying at a foreign campus of a UK university allows home students to avoid all the hustle involved with securing a UK student visa.

A study by the UK Higher Education International Unit (HEIU) shows student satisfaction with UK higher education is very high at 91%.[6] Student satisfaction ratings for the UK were the highest in all the key aspects of the student experience, including overall satisfaction, learning, living, support and arrival experience. There is a variety of reasons why the UK is a leading destination for international students.

These include the following:

- **Quality of education:** Britain is a world leader in international education. A study by the UK HEIU shows that for learning experience, the UK international student experience is ahead of other rival destinations (though closely followed by the US).[7] When it comes to the learning experience, the UK holds a remarkable advantage in two main areas: (a) academic expertise and research and; (b) technology, library and education facilities.

  In this respect, the quality of education is an area where the UK has established a comparative advantage over other international destinations for higher education.[8] Students are also attracted to the wider range of high quality courses on offer at UK institutions.

- **Institutional reputation:** The reputation of the selected university is a principal factor underpinning the decision of international students coming to the UK.[9] In fact, the study by the UK HEIU showed that most students rated institutional reputation and specific courses of study as their most significant decision-making factors.[10]

- **Diverse student experience:** Students are attracted by the rich and culturally diverse student experience that they can have. From the urban experience in major cities like London, Birmingham, Cardiff, Leeds and Edinburgh, to historic counties like Hampshire and Warwickshire, the UK has much to offer. Moreover, students will make lifelong friends from all over the world, as Britain has a long history of welcoming international students. The UK university experience gives international students the opportunity to gain their higher education qualification whilst also being exposed to different cultures and new experiences.

- **Work while you study:** The UK is very appealing for international students because of the opportunity to work while studying. If you are studying for a degree-level qualification at a recognised institution, you can work for a maximum of 20 hours a week during term time. During vacation periods, students can work full-time.

This is very advantageous as it allows students to earn money to cover their living expenses. It allows students to develop work experience and gain meaningful employability skills before they graduate.

Other reasons cited for coming to the UK to study include job opportunities, earning potential, family ties, cost of living, availability of scholarships and bursaries, personal safety, English speaking, commonwealth links, and opportunities for further study.

Here are some reasons cited by other international students:

 What former students say:

"I came to the UK because it was a family tradition. I was a fourth generation member of my family to study in the UK. Additionally, it was advantageous for my intended career path given the historical nexus between the UK and Sri Lankan legal systems."
– Niroshan (Sri Lanka)

"The key reason I chose to study in UK was because of the international work atmosphere that this place provides. Studying with a class full of students brings a whole other perspective in discussions."
– Ajay (India)

"Global reach, education quality, reputation, English language and due to a friend's advice." **– Adham (Lebanon)**

"I visited the UK before, and I liked the country. Also, I liked the country's culture and wished to know more about it." **– Alex (Russia)**

> "The UK, and Europe generally, have a high standard of education. It is probably rated higher than even some American education facilities. I also liked the fact that the system is very similar to that in Uganda allowing for students sitting for exams both under Cambridge and the Uganda National Examination Board to convert their grades without having to take a bridging exam like the GMAT (usually required by American universities)." – **Angela (Uganda)**

Although the UK remains a highly favoured destination for international students, there are concerns that other countries (e.g. Australia) are slowly catching up.

In September 2018, it was reported that university groups were lobbying the government to make the UK more welcoming to international students. There were calls for the government to grant students the right to stay and work in the UK when they complete their studies (as they could before the rules were changed in 2012). University groups highlight the contributions made by international students to the UK economy. It is estimated that spending by international students is worth around £26bn, supporting approximately 200,000 jobs.

Prevailing rules in September 2018 allow students to stay in the UK after graduating if they secure a graduate level job or an internship or they apply to set up a business in the UK. However, these rules are restrictive, with thresholds on how much graduates must earn, time limits for moving into work and sponsorship requirements. It remains to be seen whether the UK government will take steps to make the rules less restrictive. A move by the government to make the rules more flexible would be welcomed and would help to maintain the UK's reputation as a highly favoured destination for international students.

Intense competition for graduate jobs

"Every morning in Africa, a gazelle wakes up, it knows it must outrun the fastest lion or it will be killed. Every morning in Africa, a lion wakes up. It knows it must run faster than the slowest gazelle, or it will starve. It doesn't matter whether you're the lion or a gazelle – when the sun comes up, you'd better be running."
– African proverb

"Research has shown the assumption that entry to university automatically confers access to the upper echelons of any career, which is the essence of social mobility, is largely mythical."
– HECSU/ AGCAS[11]

The graduate market today is extremely competitive. Students embarking on their university journeys need to realise that the graduate landscape ahead of them will probably be more challenging than they expected. Students should be under no illusion that a degree qualification from a UK university alone is sufficient to guarantee a good career after graduation.

Over the past decade, there has been a gradual increase in the number of graduates. The UK Office for National Statistics (ONS) shows that in 2017, there were 14 million graduates in the UK. As the pool of graduates has increased, competition for graduate schemes has intensified.

One trend that illustrates the intensity of competition is that recruiters have become more demanding about candidates having prior experience. Many leading employers won't even consider a candidate if they have no relevant work experience.

International students seeking employment in the UK face additional challenges, as any prospective employers would have to obtain the relevant work permits/visa. In reality, this means that job applications from international students need to be exceptional. Recruiters would need to be convinced that it is justifiable to incur all the administrative and financial burdens of employing an international student over other UK/EU candidates.

Most international students surveyed for this book stated that they found it more difficult to find a job than they had expected, as the following quotes indicate:

 What former students say:

"Job hunting was harder in the UK than I expected; in my case, the reputation of the university didn't make any difference."
– **Alex (Russia)**

"Getting jobs in the UK was more difficult than I had expected."
– **Alok (India)**

"As international students from China, it was very hard for us to look for a job in the UK. The university's reputation or ranking did not really help." – **Jianqiao (China)**

It is worth noting that although most of the graduates surveyed found it difficult finding jobs in the UK, some of them were eventually successful.

Despite the intense competition in the jobs market, there are many reasons to be optimistic. The prospects for graduates are more favourable as they are more likely to be employed, work in more high-skilled roles and earn more compared to non-graduates.

The ONS also found that graduates with undergraduate degrees in medicine or engineering were the most likely to be employed and had the highest average gross annual pay in 2017.

The Institute of Student Employers reports that it expects employers to increase their graduate job vacancies by 11% in 2018 (an additional 1,423 graduate jobs).

According to *High Fliers Research*, in 2018, the biggest growth in graduate opportunities was expected to come from engineering, accounting and professional services and public sector organisations. Although the Brexit vote has weighed down on recruitment, there now seems to be a return to a relatively normal state and a more positive mood from employers.

There is still a high demand for the right talent, and students with the right set of skills should feel confident that there are plenty of graduate opportunities available.

International students need to realise that they have unique qualities that may make them more attractive to potential employers. In today's global marketplace, many organisations do business in more than one country. These organisations will seek to employ graduates who have an increased cultural awareness and an international outlook. International students will have many of the qualities that are highly sought after by employers such as fluency in other languages and knowledge of foreign markets.

Furthermore, the experience of living and studying abroad helps students develop confidence and maturity. It also shows that they can adapt to unfamiliar environments. All these qualities are highly desirable by employers, which puts international students at an advantage when applying for jobs.

There are many other reasons international students can be optimistic about their future prospects. The insights and tips offered in this book will help students to plan their career journeys so that they are best placed to take advantage of all the graduate opportunities on offer.

PART ONE

Before university

CHAPTER 1

Choosing your university – it is important where you study

The university you attend can be a significant factor in determining your graduate career prospects, so it is important to understand the different universities in the UK. There are over one hundred and sixty institutions to choose from, and they can be vastly different, making it difficult to make a meaningful and informed decision.

Prospective students may not always appreciate how diverse UK universities can be and how the university you attend could be a significant factor in career prospects. Competition to attract international students is intense; with many universities adopting targeted marketing campaigns or using education agents in different countries.

Consequently, prospective students end up being influenced by these direct recruitment campaigns, proactive education agents, as well as family and friends. However, these influences may not always reflect the best choices available to them.

I recall my initial choices for undergraduate study were primarily influenced by the universities that actively marketed and recruited at my school. I was fortunate to have visited the UK before I started university, which enabled me to undertake further research. I then realised that I had not made the best choices for university and had sold myself short.

Eventually, I changed my university selection, applied through the UCAS clearing process, and got accepted at a university with a better reputation than my initial choices. The importance of the university I attended became clear when I applied for vacation placements and graduate roles during my penultimate year and final year.

Here are some of the factors that other international students considered in choosing their university:

What former students say:

"University reputations as well as course ranking were important factors for me when I chose the university. At the time, I did not consider other factors. For instance, I did not know how important links to employers would be." – **Jianqiao (China)**

"Reputation, ranking of the university and links to employers were important to me. I did not think the location of the university was a big factor." – **Alok (India)**

"Cost was the first consideration, closely followed by reputation. As an international student the costs for education abroad is a large commitment. I was fortunate enough to have parents financially support me but the cost was still a concern." - **Nkatha (Kenya)**

"The universities I picked for both my undergrad and post-graduate degrees were mainly chosen on the basis of global ranking for the

> *courses that I was looking to specialize in. Luckily, both were also situated 25 minutes outside of the city, London, so not too expensive in terms of accommodation, but also easy access to the city."*
> **– Angela (Uganda)**

In this section, we will look at the current higher education system and the different universities available. We shall then look at the key factors that affect graduate career prospects so you have a good understanding about making your university choices. Ideally, this will enable you to make your choice based on universities that align to your career objectives and help you maximise your career prospects.

Understanding the university system

The UK higher education sector was reformed significantly in the 1990s. Before 1992, UK higher education was characterised by two key features: (a) traditional universities, which were research-led institutions with degree-awarding powers and; (b) polytechnics, which provided courses in more technical or vocational-orientated subjects but did not have full degree-awarding powers.

In 1992, this distinction was removed, and all higher education institutions were granted university status and degree-awarding powers. Following these reforms, various universities banded together to form networks and associations that would advance their interests with government and other stakeholders.

To make it easier to understand the current higher education system, I have categorised UK universities in two ways:

(1) historical categorisation (based on when they were founded) and;

(2) whether they belong to specific associations.

We look at these in more detail below.

1. Historical categories

(a) Ancient universities
The ancient universities are the seven oldest universities in the UK, founded between the 12th and 16th century in England, Scotland and Ireland. The earliest is the University of Oxford in 1096 and the latest is the University of Dublin in 1592.

- University of Oxford
- University of Cambridge
- University of St Andrews
- University of Glasgow
- University of Aberdeen
- University of Edinburgh
- University of Dublin

(b) Red brick universities
Red Brick originally referred to the civic universities that were given charters in the 19th century in the major industrial cities of the UK. The term is now used more broadly to refer to British universities founded in the late 19th and early 20th centuries in major cities.

The original Red Brick universities were:

- University of Birmingham
- University of Liverpool
- University of Manchester
- University of Leeds
- University of Sheffield
- University of Bristol

The original Red Brick institutions were then joined by a number of other universities that were given a charter between 1900 and 1963.

• Aberystwyth University	• University of Newcastle Upon Tyne
• Bangor University	
• Cardiff University	• University of Nottingham
• University of Dundee	• Queen's University Belfast
• University of Hull	• University of Reading
• University of Wales Trinity St David	• University of Southampton
	• University of Swansea
• University of Leicester	

(c) Plate glass universities

Plate glass universities were the next group of universities that were granted royal charter between 1963 and 1992.

• Aston University	• Lancaster University
• University of Bath	• Loughborough University
• University of Bradford	• University of Stirling
• Cranfield University	• University of Strathclyde
• University of East Anglia	• University of Surrey
• University of Essex	• University of Sussex
• Heriot-Watt University	• University of Warwick
• Keele University	• University of Ulster
• University of Kent	• University of York

(d) New universities

The term new (or post-1992) universities refer to those institutions that started out as polytechnics, providing courses in more technical or vocational-orientated subjects. These institutions were later granted university status from 1992 onwards.

• Anglia Ruskin	• Manchester Metropolitan University
• Birmingham City University	
• Bournemouth University	• Middlesex University
• University of Brighton	• Northumbria University
• University of Central Lancashire	• Nottingham Trent University
• Coventry University	• Oxford Brookes University
• De Montfort University	• University of Plymouth
• University of East London	• University of Portsmouth
• University of Greenwich	• Sheffield Hallam University
• University of Hertfordshire	• University of South Wales
• University of Huddersfield	• Staffordshire University
• Kingston University	• University of Sunderland
• Leeds Beckett University	• Teesside University
• University of Lincoln	• University of the West of England
• Liverpool John Moores University	
• London Metropolitan University	• University of West London
	• University of Westminster
• London South Bank University	• University of Wolverhampton

Since 1992, many other institutions were granted university status, including some that were not polytechnics. They include:

• Arden University	• University of Cumbria
• Edinburgh Napier University	• University of Derby
• University of Abertay Dundee	• Edge Hill University
• Bath Spa University	• Falmouth University
• Glasgow Caledonian University	• University of Gloucestershire
• University of the West of Scotland	• Glyndŵr University
	• Harper Adams University
• The Robert Gordon University	• University of Law
• University of the Arts London	• Leeds Trinity University
• The Arts University Bournemouth	• Liverpool Hope University
	• Newman University
• University of Bedfordshire	• University of Northampton
• University College Birmingham	• Norwich University of the Arts
• Bishop Grosseteste University	• Queen Margaret University
• University of Bolton	• University of Roehampton
• BPP University	• Regent's University London
• Buckinghamshire New University	• Royal Agricultural University
	• Southampton Solent University
• Canterbury Christ Church University	• University of St Mark & St John
• Cardiff Metropolitan University	• University of Winchester
• University of Chester	• University of Worcester
• University of Chichester	• York St John University
• University for the Creative Arts	

2. Associations

Certain universities banded together to form groups or associations that could better represent their collective interests, influence public policy and help share best practice. The main groups are described below:

(a) The Russell Group

The Russell Group is a coalition of twenty-four research-led institutions, which encompasses some of the oldest and most prestigious higher education institutions in the UK. It was formed in 1994 and named after the hotel where the group had its first informal meetings. Russell group members receive a significant portion of research funding. In fact, it is estimated that Russell Group universities get half of all funding for the entire higher education sector. The group is perceived to represent the leading institutions, resulting in highly competitive application processes for places at Russell Group universities. The Russell group consists of the following universities:

• University of Birmingham	• University of Manchester
• University of Bristol	• Newcastle University
• University of Cambridge	• University of Nottingham
• Cardiff University	• University of Oxford
• Durham University	• Queen Mary University of London
• University of Edinburgh	
• University of Exeter	• Queen's University Belfast
• University of Glasgow	• University of Sheffield
• Imperial College London	• University of Southampton

• King's College London	• University College London
• University of Leeds	• University of Warwick
• University of Liverpool	• University of York
• London School of Economics	

(b) University Alliance

The University Alliance (initially known as the *Alliance of Non-Aligned Universities*) is an association of UK universities that was formed in 2006. It is comprised of professional and technical universities which seek to drive growth and innovation through teaching, research and enterprise activity, focussing specifically on links with business and industry and applied research with real-world relevance.

• University of Brighton	• Nottingham Trent University
• University of Central Lancashire	• The Open University
• Coventry University	• Oxford Brookes University
• University of Greenwich	• University of Portsmouth
• University of Hertfordshire	• University of Salford
• University of Huddersfield	• Sheffield Hallam University
• Kingston University	• University of South Wales
• Liverpool John Moores University	• Teesside University
• Manchester Metropolitan University	• University of the West of England

(c) MillionPlus

MillionPlus is a network of universities that seeks to promote the interests of modern universities. All its members are institutions that were granted university status from 1992 onwards, many of which have long histories as polytechnics and colleges. Current membership includes:

• Abertay University	• Leeds Trinity University
• Anglia Ruskin University	• London Metropolitan University
• Bath Spa University	
• University of Bedfordshire	• London South Bank University
• University of Bolton	• Middlesex University
• Canterbury Christ Church University	• Southampton Solent University
	• Staffordshire University
• University of Cumbria	• University of Sunderland
• University of East London	• University of West London
• Edinburgh Napier University	• University of the West of Scotland
• University of the Highlands and Islands	

(d) The 1994 Group

The 1994 Group was an association of smaller research-focused universities, formed to defend the interests of its members (in response to the creation of the Russell Group). The group's mission was to represent the interests of its members through dialogue with government, funding bodies, and other higher education interest groups.

The group initially consisted of seventeen universities, but the group started to struggle from 2012, as some of its members left and joined the Russell Group. The 1994 Group eventually dissolved in 2013. Membership of the group used to include:

• University of Bath	• Loughborough University
• Birkbeck, University of London	• University of Manchester Institute of Science and Technology (UMIST)
• Durham University	
• University of East Anglia	
• University of Essex	• Queen Mary, University
• University of Exeter	• University of Reading
• Goldsmiths, University of London	• Royal Holloway,
	• University of St Andrews
• Institute of Education, University of London	• SOAS, University of London
• University of Lancaster	• University of Surrey
• University of Leicester	• University of Sussex
• London School of Economics	• University of Warwick
	• University of York

Why the university you attend matters

Attending university in the UK is a very expensive venture. For UK or EU nationals, universities in England can charge up to a maximum of £9,250 per year in tuition fees. For international students, tuition fees alone can range from £10,000 to £38,000 per annum.[12]

On top of this, you have the cost of living, which is estimated to be around £12,200 per annum. If you study in London, your budget would be considerably more expensive. The costs will often feel more astronomical during your first few weeks in the UK, as you compare your expenditure in Sterling to your local currency. You may easily find yourself thinking about other ways that you could have invested in your future, e.g. launch a start-up business, fund a property investment, etc.

It is not just a financial investment; it's also an investment of your time (three years or more at the prime of your life). As such, you want to ensure that you're making the right university choice and that it is a worthwhile investment in your future.

In this chapter, we shall look at four key factors you should consider when choosing your university:

- Reputation;
- Rankings;
- Teaching excellence and student outcomes;
- How it improves your employment prospects.

Taking these factors into account when choosing your university will help you to maximise your career opportunities.

Reputation

The reputation of the university you attend can have a significant impact on your graduate career prospects. A survey by *QS World University Rankings* showed the importance of reputation, with over 60% of students interviewed stating that it was important for a university to be internationally recognised in order to improve their employment prospects.[13]

The oldest institutions like Oxford and Cambridge in the UK or the Ivy League universities in the US have illustrious reputations that give their graduates considerable advantage in securing prestigious careers.

The significance of reputation on graduate employment prospects is more evident when you look at the universities targeted for recruitment by employers. Research shows that employers actively marketed their graduate vacancies at an average of 21 UK universities.[14] Eighty-eight percent of the top 25 universities targeted by the largest number of leading employers[15] in 2017/18 were Russell Group universities (see table 1).

The evidence of leading employers targeting their recruitment at Russell Group universities is hardly surprising. I recall from my undergraduate experience that employers were very selective, which meant that recruitment events like open days and recruitment presentations were limited to students from specific universities.

Table 1: Universities Targeted by the Largest Number of Top Employers in 2017-2018

1. Manchester	14. London Imperial College
2. Birmingham	15. Sheffield
3. Warwick	16. London School of Economics
4. Bristol	17. Southampton
5. University College London	18. Loughborough
6. Cambridge	19. King's College London
7. Leeds	20. Newcastle
8. Nottingham	21. York
9. Oxford	22. Cardiff
10. Durham	23. Leicester
11. Bath	24. Glasgow
12. Exeter	25. Liverpool
13. Edinburgh	

Source: The Graduate Market in 2018

If you are an international student, you would also need to consider the reputation of certain UK universities in your home country, particularly if your intention is to return home to launch your career. Some universities are more recognised in certain countries due to historical links and well-established alumni networks. It is worth doing research in your home country to understand whether any universities have well-established reputations.

If you are interested in a specific career path, research the educational backgrounds of notable practitioners or personalities. For instance, if you are interested in a legal career in your home country, speak to lawyers and do some online research about the biographies of prominent lawyers and judges. You might discover a preference for certain universities. You can also enquire with prospective universities whether they have an established alumni network in your home country.

Rankings and league tables

"People are suckers for league tables, be they of wealth, beauty, fame – or institutions of higher education." - **The Economist**[16]

League tables have become increasingly popular tools for deciding which institution to attend. Whilst they can be useful sources of information about university performance, applicants should not base their university choice solely on university league tables or rankings.

It is important to note that league tables measure universities differently, emphasising different factors. For instance, most rankings use research quality as a key metric but place less emphasis on teaching quality, as it is more difficult to measure.

However, teaching quality is a crucial metric and arguably has more of an impact on the quality of education and outcomes for graduates.

I would advise applicants to use league tables after other sources of information have been considered. For instance, after you have considered reputation and employability factors and you have a shortlist of, say, seven universities you think are evenly matched. Here, rankings may help you focus your search to consider other factors that can narrow your list further (e.g. cost and location).

Global and National Rankings

There are three global league tables that could be considered the most influential – the Times Higher Education, QS World University Rankings and the Shanghai Ranking. Before we look at these influential global rankings, take note that research excellence is a major factor influencing a university's ranking.

Unfortunately, the focus on research excellence may come at the expense of the quality of teaching – which has more of an impact on outcomes for graduates. We look at these in more detail below.

(a) **Times Higher Education World University Rankings** – Since 2004, the Times Higher Education ("THE") has published annual world university rankings in partnership with QS. In 2009, THE ended its partnership with QS and developed a new methodology in collaboration with Thomson Reuters.

THE World University Rankings is one of the most influential university rankings listing the top 1,000 universities in the world. It assesses research-intensive institutions on their core missions, including research, teaching, international outlook and knowledge transfer. The 2018 rankings for best universities were led for the first time by two UK universities – University of Oxford (#1) and the University of Cambridge (#2). Imperial College London was the only other UK institution to feature in the top ten world rankings.

THE also lists the top universities in the UK (including their corresponding world rankings), making it easy for comparison against other universities around the world. This can be useful if you are trying to choose between universities in different countries. You can filter searches to show you university rankings based on subjects.

Rankings based on other areas of interest to university applicants are also available, e.g. cheapest cities to live, best universities by region, and top accommodation halls. The website has lots of information that university applicants will find useful and worth browsing as part of your research – *https://www. timeshighereducation.com/world-university-rankings.*

(b) **QS World University Rankings** – Another leading higher education league table is the annual world university ranking by Quacquarelli Symonds (QS). QS Rankings assess performance on what it considers the core aspects of a university's mission – research, teaching, employability and internationalisation. Four UK universities featured in the top ten for the 2018 rankings – Cambridge, Oxford, University College London and Imperial College London.

On its website, *https://www.topuniversities.com/*, you can filter the rankings based on country, region, study level and subjects of interest. There is a comparison tool on the website which provides a single view of selected institutions with metrics that may be of interest, including ranking history, average fees, research activity, size, and number of international students. You can obtain detailed reports for undergraduate or postgraduate study, if you register your details.

(c) **Shanghai Ranking** – The Shanghai Ranking or Academic Ranking of World Universities (ARWU) is another popular annual league table. It was first published by Shanghai Jiao Tong University in 2003.

Since 2009, it has been published by an independent organisation – the Shanghai Ranking Consultancy. The rankings assess four key factors: quality of education, research output, quality of faculty and per capita performance. You can filter searches on its website by country, which allows you to compare national rankings alongside the world rank. In 2017 rankings, three UK institutions featured in the top twenty rankings – Cambridge, Oxford and University College London. You can view the ARWU rankings on its website – *http://www.shanghairanking.com/*.

Besides global rankings, there are national league tables that prospective applicants may find useful:

(d) **The Complete University Guide (CUG)** – The CUG ranks UK universities in 70 subjects, sourcing its data from sources in the public domain. The measures used for the CUG rankings include: entry standards, research quality, student satisfaction and graduate prospects. You can filter results in the CUG league table by subject, year, regions and university association. The CUG rankings are accessible via the following website – *https://www. thecompleteuniversityguide.co.uk/league-tables/*.

(e) **The Guardian University League Table** – Every year, the *Guardian* publishes a university league table based on factors considered most important to students, including: how much students will benefit from teaching, whether other students liked the university or subject, and chances of getting a good job. You can access the university league table via the Guardian website – *https://www. theguardian.com/education/universityguide*.

Teaching excellence and student outcomes

The *Teaching Excellence and Student Outcomes Framework* (TEF) is a new initiative that aims to improve the higher education experience by measuring factors that students care about – teaching quality, learning environment and what students do afterwards. The TEF is a government-backed assessment of the quality of undergraduate teaching in higher education providers in England. Institutions from other parts of the UK can opt-in.

Given the deficiency of most league tables focusing on research excellence, the TEF ratings are a beneficial source of information for prospective students. The final ratings are awarded by the TEF panel, which includes students and academics. The first TEF results were published in 2017 and the awards are valid for up to three years. The table below describes the different TEF ratings available.

Table 2: TEF ratings and descriptions

TEF Rating	Description
Gold	Awarded where the TEF Panel has judged that the institution delivers consistently outstanding teaching, learning and outcomes for its students and of the highest quality found in the UK Higher Education sector.
	The award considers the following factors:
	• The achievement of consistently outstanding outcomes for students from all backgrounds – particularly regarding retention and progression to graduate level employment and further study.
	• Course design and assessment provide scope for outstanding levels of stretch that ensures all students are significantly challenged to achieve their full potential and acquire knowledge, skills and understanding that are most highly valued by employers.
	• Optimum levels of contact time, including outstanding personalised provision, secure the highest levels of engagement and active commitment to learning and study from students.

TEF Rating	Description
	• Outstanding physical and digital resources are actively and consistently used by students to enhance learning. • Students are consistently and frequently engaged with developments from the forefront of research, scholarship or practice, and are consistently and frequently involved in these activities. • An institutional culture that facilitates, recognises and rewards excellent teaching is well-embedded.
Silver	Awarded where the TEF panel has judged that the institution delivers high quality teaching, learning and outcomes for its students; and it consistently exceeds the rigorous national quality requirements for UK Higher Education. The following are given consideration: • Achievement of excellent outcomes for students – particularly with regards to retention and progression to graduate level employment and further study. • Course design and assessment practices provide scope for high levels of stretch that ensures all students are significantly challenged and acquire knowledge, skills and understanding that are highly valued by employers. • Appropriate levels of contact time, including personalised provision, secure high levels of engagement and commitment to learning and study from students.

TEF Rating	Description
	• High quality physical and digital resources are used by students to enhance learning. • Students are engaged with developments from the forefront of research, scholarship or practice, and are sometimes involved in these activities. • An institutional culture that facilitates, recognises and rewards excellent teaching has been implemented.
Bronze	Awarded where the TEF panel has judged that the institution delivers teaching, learning and outcomes for students that meet the rigorous national quality requirements for UK Higher Education. The award takes the following factors: • Achievement of good outcomes for most of its students. However, the institution is likely to be significantly below benchmark in one or more areas – especially in relation to retention and progression to graduate level employment and further study. • Course design and assessment practices provide sufficient stretch that ensures most students make progress and acquire knowledge, skills and understanding that are valued by employers. • Sufficient levels of contact time, including personalised provision, secures good engagement and commitment to learning and study from most students.

TEF Rating	Description
	• Physical and digital resources are used by students to further learning. • Students are occasionally engaged with developments from the forefront of research, scholarship or practice, and are occasionally involved in these activities. • An institutional culture that facilitates, recognises and rewards excellent teaching has been introduced.
Provisional	Awarded where the TEF Panel has judged that the institution meets the rigorous national quality requirements for UK higher education but is unable to be assessed for a TEF rating of gold, silver or bronze due to insufficient data.

Source: Department of Education

There was a mixed reaction to TEF ratings when first published in 2017. Some institutions have claimed TEF ratings are subjective and do not provide an accurate assessment of teaching quality; whilst others called it a godsend that would bring long-term benefits for students and universities.

For prospective students, TEF ratings are a helpful source of information because of the focus on teaching quality and other metrics that matter more to students. Increasingly, students are paying more attention to the quality of teaching when making their choices for university.

Universities are also focusing more on improving teaching quality (e.g. ensuring that academics make themselves more accessible to students and increasing the quality of feedback provided on student assessments). Smaller and lesser known universities are distinguishing themselves from the older prestigious institutions by providing better teaching quality for students.

TEF ratings for various institutions can be viewed on the Office for Students "OFS" website (in the TEF Outcomes section).

The OFS is a government-backed regulator for the higher education sector in England. It promotes student interests and aims to ensure that students get a high-quality education that prepares them for their future. In addition to viewing TEF ratings for individual institutions, you can also access: (a) the TEF Panel's rationale for its rating; and (b) the evidence submitted by the institution.

These two reports will help you understand what activities a university is undertaking to improve student experience. You can access the OFS website via the following link – *https://www.officeforstudents.org.uk/*.

Employment prospects

When you are choosing a university, it is also important to consider how active it is in enhancing the employment prospects of its students. This is often referred to as the employability factors.

Employability can be a vague term which most students may not understand. In simple terms, employability is about enhancing career or employment prospects. Therefore, prospective students need to understand how a particular university will support them in establishing their careers.

Employability in this context refers to a set of skills and personal attributes that make students more likely to gain employment and be successful in their chosen occupations[17]. Employability also includes entrepreneurship, which is increasingly becoming more recognised as a career choice for students.

Employability is not just about securing a job; it's about equipping students for career success throughout their lifetimes. In today's competitive graduate recruitment market, employers seek to recruit "work-ready" graduates who have job-specific skills besides a university qualification. A degree is no longer sufficient in itself to guarantee a successful graduate career. Therefore, to have the competitive edge in the job market, you will need to develop your employability throughout your time at university.

The good universities will have invested in programmes and initiatives that will help develop your employability throughout your time at university. These universities ensure that students gain not only an academic qualification but also equipped with the skills they need to succeed in the workforce. These universities will have developed strategies that seek to deliver greater graduate outcomes. Such strategies often entail working closely with leading employers and having a well-resourced university career service that supports students with career development throughout their time at university. They may even have programmes tailored to developing the employability of overseas students.

Some of the newer universities appear to be focusing a lot more on employability-enhancing initiatives, which is making them more attractive than some Russell Group universities that may focus more on teaching and research. So just because a university is old, prestigious, or outstanding in its research, does not always translate into employability for its graduates. It should also be noted that whilst employability might feature prominently in mission statements, this does not mean that there are coherent strategies embedded in the student experience.

When it comes to assessing the employability factors for particular universities, I would recommend you focus on the following key areas:

(a) availability of industrial placements,

(b) internships and work experience opportunities;

(c) the strength of university links with industry and leading employers (including whether these partnerships are being used to create opportunities for students);

(d) the university careers service;

(e) breadth of extra-curricular activity; and

(f) Support provided for entrepreneurship activity (i.e., whether supporting entrepreneurship is a core part of the university's mission and strategy).

(a) Industrial placements

Employability is greatly enhanced when students can develop practical and meaningful work experience whilst learning. A degree course with an industrial placement is an ideal way of achieving this. An industrial placement is a work experience assignment with an employer that forms part of your degree course at university.

It is sometimes referred to as a "sandwich" placement because it takes place between the penultimate and final year of study. The duration of a placement can typically vary from 9 to 13 months. Some universities will improve your employment prospects through their strong connections to industry. For instance, you may find that universities are affiliated with certain industries/

employers and will actively assist you in finding a work placement. Placements will greatly enhance your career prospects in the following ways:

- Firstly, they will give you valuable work experience, without which you would struggle to secure a graduate career. Getting meaningful work experience is almost as difficult as finding a graduate role. Most recruiters even discourage applicants without previous work experience from applying for their graduate programmes.

  An industrial placement allows you to gain that all-important work experience as part of your degree. It will also help you apply the knowledge you have gained from university in a real-world environment. You will also gain vital new skills in readiness for the world of work (e.g. teamwork, problem solving, communication, organising and planning).

- Placements are often viewed by recruiters as a more meaningful assessment of a graduate's potential, outside of the traditional selection process. A placement can be considered an extended job interview where your skills, personality, and fit within the company can be properly assessed. At the end of your placement, you may get offered a graduate job or get fast-tracked in the application process for the organisation's graduate programme.

- Placements are a great opportunity to build your professional network. Even if you decide not to pursue a long-term career with the organisation that provided you with the placement, the contacts you gain may help open new doors of opportunity with other employers.

- Earning potential during your career can be enhanced by undertaking a placement. There is evidence from the Department of Education[18] that placement students are more likely to be employed and more likely to have higher earnings than students who did not undertake placements.

- Undertaking a placement as part of your degree will also help you make better informed choices about your future career. You may find out more about niche areas or specialisms you were not aware of within a particular industry sector. For instance, you might pursue a civil engineering degree but have no idea about the sub-disciplines like construction, transportation, structural, environmental, etc. Alternatively, you might be a business student but not sure about what industries you would be most interested in, e.g. financial services, oil and gas, and automotive manufacturing. A placement would give you more insights into these niche areas and help you make a more informed choice about your career direction.

During your placement you might discover that you're more interested in a field of expertise that you would never have considered if it wasn't for that placement. Equally, you may realise that you dislike working in a particular specialism and decide to change your career direction altogether. A placement will go a long way to help you make these decisions.

Factors to consider when researching courses with industrial placements

When you're exploring prospective universities, research the availability of placements as part of the degree programme. If industrial placements are offered as part of a course programme, check to see if they are guaranteed.

Some universities create misleading impressions about the availability of industrial placements, and your chances of securing one might be non-existent. The last thing you want is to find that the availability of placements is limited for one reason or another (e.g. for only UK/EU nationals or for research in a niche topic).

Check to see whether the placements on offer are paid opportunities. Although most placements are paid, this might not be the case for placements in the not-for-profit or public sector.

You should also enquire about the tuition fee arrangements during your placement year. Many universities will offer reduced tuition fees (50% or more) during your placement year. The university may also offer some form of financial support, e.g. bursaries or grants, if the placement is unpaid.

You should also confirm whether the financial arrangements regarding placements are the same for international students as for UK/EU students. Some universities do not always make it clear that there are different requirements or arrangements that apply if you are an international student.

Also, try to assess the level of support you will have from the university during the placement period. A placement can be a challenging experience, and you may have to relocate to a new city away from the university. Making a smooth transition from a familiar university environment to work life may depend on the level of support you have available. For instance, will the university provide a tutor or careers advisor to help you settle into your new role and help you manage any emerging concerns during the placement? Your chances of success during a placement will be much higher if you get the right level of support.

Check that the placement experience will count towards your final degree results. It is also worth checking whether the placements are advantageous in achieving industry-recognised qualifications or membership in professional bodies.

Recap: Important points to remember when considering industrial placements

Advantages of an industrial placement on your career:

- To gain valuable work experience, without which most graduates find it difficult to secure graduate jobs.

- To get "a foot in the door" with employers of interest. Many recruiters view placements as extended job interviews and are more likely to offer graduate jobs to students who have done placements with them.

- For increased earning potential over the course of your career.

- To build your professional network.

- To make better informed decisions about specialist or niche areas to develop your career.

Factors to consider when researching courses with industrial placements:

- Check whether the placement is guaranteed as part of your degree course (and that there are no restrictions).

- Confirm whether placements are paid opportunities.

- Check whether financial arrangements for the placement vary depending on your status (i.e. are there different arrangements for UK/EU students compared to non-UK/EU?).

- Assess the overall level of support you will have from the university during the placement.

- Confirm whether the placement counts towards your degree results.

(b) Internships and vacation work

You can also gain work experience through internships and work experience schemes during the winter or summer vacation periods. These work experience schemes will help you develop valuable employability skills and also equip you to manage the transition from study to work.

You may also develop a mentoring relationship with an employer through which you can gain continued support with your career development. The duration of these schemes can vary, ranging from one week (e.g. mini-pupillages for law students) to three months (vacation schemes).

(c) Links with industry and leading employers

Good universities will collaborate with industry and leading employers not only to further their own academic research interests but also to enhance the employability of their students. Close collaboration between universities and employers can create opportunities for students to gain work experience or attend networking events where they can interact directly with employers.

(d) The University Careers service

A university careers service (sometimes referred to as a careers development centre) provides advice and a range of services geared towards helping students to build their employability skills and make the most of their time at university. They offer a broad range of services such as job application clinics, CV workshops, and assessment centres. Career advisers may help you with job hunting strategies, interview techniques, etc.

Although most universities have a careers service, the quality and range of services provided can vary significantly – which can make a difference to your graduate career prospects. When I talk to graduates, this is one area where you find contrasting experiences. Some say they were *"completely let down"* by their university careers service, whilst others will cite the fantastic support they received and even credit their success in finding a graduate position to their university careers service.

One thing former graduates agree on, though, is that students need to be more proactive and not rely on their careers service to take the initiative.

(e) Extra-curricular activities and community engagement

Employers value well-rounded graduates with wide-ranging interests and hobbies. Active involvement in extra-curricular activity through university societies and sports clubs helps students to develop many of the "soft" skills that employers wish to see in prospective employees, including communication, teamwork, problem solving, and resilience.

Volunteering opportunities through not-for-profit organisations help students demonstrate their passion and initiative. Universities that have an abundance of societies, sports clubs and other volunteering activities will give you tremendous opportunities to get involved in extra-curricular activities, and the chance to have fun and make a lot of friends.

(f) Entrepreneurship

Universities have tended to focus more on helping students find graduate careers with existing employers and less on helping them to launch their own businesses. This has often meant that the university careers services have not been focussed or resourced to support self-employment or entrepreneurship.

A 2017 report by the *Centre for Entrepreneurs* highlighted that universities were not doing enough to support entrepreneurship.

It is no wonder that the start-up rate for graduates is quite low despite the entrepreneurial aspirations and potential of many students before university.

University can be the ideal time to develop enterprise skills and attributes such as idea generation, design thinking, innovation, problem solving and practical action. As a student, you could also gain exposure to a variety of activities, such as business competitions through which you could build a network of contacts and even meet your future business partners and co-founders.

Remember, some of the most successful companies started off as collaborations between students at university. *Google* started as a research project by Larry Page and Sergey Brin, while *Yahoo* was started Jerry Yang and David Filo when they were graduate students.

If you harbour entrepreneurial intentions, then you need to establish whether the universities you are considering will help you on that journey and turn your aspirations into a reality.

Even if you don't have intentions of starting your own business, developing your entrepreneurial skills will be advantageous for graduate careers. The concept of "intrapreneurship" (displaying entrepreneurial attributes in an established company) is attractive to many companies as it brings many sought after skills and attributes like innovation, creativity and risk taking.

You might also not realise you are a future entrepreneur until you explore some of the options available. A university that has a supportive environment and start-up culture can introduce students to entrepreneurship through light-touch activities such as presentations and workshops. As you take part in these activities, develop new ideas, collaborate with other students and may discover you are a budding entrepreneur after all.

We shall explore entrepreneurship in greater detail in subsequent chapters. We shall also hear about the experiences of two successful entrepreneurs who launched their start-up ventures after university. For now, you want to ensure that the universities you consider have the right environment.

Recap: Important considerations when choosing your university:

- **Reputation of the university** – The prestige or reputation of a particular university impacts career prospects. Evidence from the graduate market shows that recruitment activity of leading employers is quite selective; with the majority of institutions targeted being Russell Group universities.

  Additionally, the prestige of the older universities could also be given more significance by employers outside the UK. Therefore, if the reputation or prestige of the university is an important consideration, you may wish to target Russell Group universities in your university applications.

- **Rankings** – The rankings from various league tables can be useful to understand the various strengths of particular institutions and how they compare against others. You need to remember that there is a lack of consistency in the metrics used by different rankings. For instance, research excellence has tended to be given significance in comparison to quality of teaching (which is more important for students).

  Therefore, consider using rankings as a rough guide to narrow your selection between institutions that appear to be evenly matched. Additionally, you could use rankings and league tables to consider other factors that may be important to you (e.g. which university is cheaper, has better social life, or cost of living).

- **Teaching Excellence Framework** – The Government's Teaching Excellence Framework is a useful resource to understand the value delivered by a particular university in relation to the quality of teaching, learning and outcomes. As traditional rankings have given more prominence to research quality, the TEF helps to provide an assessment of teaching quality – which matters more to students.

- **Employability factors** – Employability factors should weigh prominently as you select your university. At the core of employability, it is really all about how a university is preparing and supporting its students for a successful long-term career.

It should be noted that employability is one area where some of the newer and smaller universities are delivering more value for students compared to the older institutions. Therefore, you should not simply be blinded by the prestige of particular universities but also carefully consider how a particular university would deliver great value by enhancing your employability.

CHAPTER 2

How to assess universities on employability and entrepreneurship

Making an objective assessment about the employability factors discussed above is not a straightforward exercise. Consider a variety of sources before you reach any conclusion. In this chapter, we shall cover the activities you can undertake to help you make that assessment.

The Alumni network

Former graduates will be best placed to share their experiences and give you a realistic view about how a university is performing on employability factors. For instance, they can share their experiences about using the university careers service and the range of clubs and societies available. They may shed more light on the strength of the university's links with industry and give you more information about what actually goes on than you could find on the university website.

You should enquire with the university admissions team to see whether they can share the contact details of alumni you can contact. Ideally, speak to graduates who have studied the same course you're considering, as experience can vary depending on the course of study (i.e., the engineering graduates might have had a more positive experience compared to the economics graduates). These variances could be attributed to several reasons, including certain faculties being better resourced and having dedicated specialist careers advisors (which might be lacking at other faculties).

If you are interested in entrepreneurship, seek out alumni who are in the process of launching their own businesses or have already started their own businesses. If there is a university incubation centre, enquire about the level of support provided by the incubation centre. Find out about the various entry routes to get ideas backed and supported by the incubation centre (e.g. what business competitions might be linked to the incubation centre).

Campus visits

If possible, try and visit the universities you're interested in applying to. A campus visit will provide a lot of useful information you would not easily find through online research or telephone calls. You could ask to attend a university open day or even make an informal campus visit during term time.

Don't feel put off if you can't attend a formal open day as it is possible to visit most university campuses without prior arrangement. Unscheduled visits may even give you a more realistic picture of what actually happens on campus (without the sales pitch from university representatives). If you plan to visit the university outside of the formal open days, make sure you visit during term time as vacation times can be very quiet and you won't get to see much.

A campus visit will give you a real feel of the faculty you're interested in and how well-resourced it is. You can then make your own judgement about whether descriptions of "state-of-the art" facilities on the website are fact or fiction. As you tour the faculties, check out their notice boards for employer-led presentations, networking events and ongoing collaborative projects with industry.

Make sure you also check out the careers office while you're on campus. You may get sight of the careers calendar which will give you a realistic picture about the range of services offered. For instance, you might see adverts for careers fairs with a list of employers attending, employability workshops, etc. Talk to students and careers advisors and find out more about how the university careers service helps students.

Online research

University websites and brochures are a good starting point. You can use these to research the full range of services and activities that are available and relevant to employability factors discussed above.

(a) Links with industry and employers

When you are researching university websites/ brochures to understand their links with industry and employers, I would suggest you consider the following questions (this is a non-exhaustive list):

What to look out for when researching links with employers and industry

- Is there evidence of ongoing collaboration with industry through research projects or case studies with major employers?

- Is there evidence that industry leaders regularly feature as guest speakers or panellists?

- Is there evidence of ongoing partnerships between the careers service and employers to deliver skills development and career advice that is industry relevant?

- Does the academic staff work regularly with employers to ensure that course content meets their expectations about key competencies and skills?

- Are alumni involved in activities with current students (e.g. through university career events, contributing to course design, teaching and assessment, or offering work experience)? Alumni sharing their knowledge and experiences can help students to relate employability to their university experience.

- Are there programmes that match students with professional mentors?

- Are courses accredited by professional bodies?

- Are there any links between some of the courses and professional associations?

- Are there opportunities for students to attend professional/industry conferences?

(b) The Careers Service

University websites will also provide information about the breadth and depth of services provided by the university careers service. Here are some of the key questions to bear in mind when reviewing the web pages about the careers service:

 What to look out for when researching the university careers service

- Does the careers service help students find work experience schemes, including winter or summer internships, spring insight days or even find work experience on campus?

- What services are provided in relation to job and vacation scheme applications (e.g. CV workshops, application clinics, mock-interviews, assessment centre days)?

- Do they organise networking events or employer speaking events?

- Is it staffed with advisors who have a broad range of industry expertise? Some universities will have dedicated advisors within certain academic departments rather than a general service for the entire university. For instance, you may find that there are specialist advisors for the law school who understand the unique aspects of the legal sector. The more specialist advisers available, the better. You may also see biographies of individual advisors to understand their industry experience.

- Is the careers service equipped to support/advise students whose intended career paths differ slightly from the norm (e.g. those who want to start their own businesses, work abroad, or freelance)?

- Check if there is a calendar of recruitment-related activities for the year ahead or the previous year. The schedule can show you what events the careers service organises and give you some indication of what support you can expect to get.

- Do they offer tailored support for international students?

- Do they organise events to support entrepreneurship? These may include "Dragons Den" style competitions where students can pitch their start-up ideas to potential investors.

- Do they support students who may have additional barriers to employment (e.g. students with disabilities, black and ethnic minorities, women entering male-dominated fields and vice-versa)?

- How long after university will services still be available for graduates? The better universities will continue to support graduates with their careers for a period following university.

Check out the Student Crowd website (*www.studentcrowd.com/*) - Student Crowd undertook a survey of over 7,000 students to rank the top 20 universities for careers services. You can read through reviews of former students to understand how they rate their careers service. The website also includes ratings from students about university clubs and societies, which may also be useful.

(c) Entrepreneurship activity at the university

When it comes to assessing whether universities have a supportive environment for   entrepreneurship, here are some of the factors that you should consider:

i.   Entrepreneurship workshops: Enquire whether the university offers training and workshops that encourage all students (regardless of their field of study) to develop enterprising thinking. These workshops can help students gradually build their understanding about what it takes to develop a business and provide opportunity to network with like-minded colleagues.

These workshops may be made available through a variety of channels, including the careers service, individual faculties or through extracurricular events.

ii. Start-up competitions and enterprise events: Enquire about availability of competitions that allow students to pitch their ideas about start-up companies. There may also be other entrepreneur events where students can present their ideas to business advisors and get tips about how to develop their ideas further. Start-up competitions may also be the entry route to a university-led incubation centre that may help launch a viable business.

iii. University-operated incubation centres: Incubation centres help new start-ups develop by providing the ecosystem and infrastructure where innovative ideas can be nurtured and developed into viable businesses. Entrepreneurs need tremendous support in the form of mentoring, financing and networking opportunities to get their businesses off the ground. Incubation centres help provide this vital support structure.

However, the analysis by the *Centre for Entrepreneurs* indicates that incubation centres are only available to graduates at 37% of universities. You should check whether the universities you are interested in house their own incubation centres and the extent to which it supports projects/ideas from students and graduates. Some university-led incubation centres may only support external ventures rather than start-up ideas from its students or graduates.

iv. Organisational environment: You need to consider whether the prevailing institutional environment and culture is favourable to student enterprise and entrepreneurship. In other words, consider whether there is evidence that the university leadership is committed to driving and supporting entrepreneurship. Here is a non-exhaustive list of things you could consider:

What to look out for when assessing the organisational environment:

- Check the university corporate plan to understand whether promoting entrepreneurship is a key part of the university's strategic agenda and mission. If the university has a vision to place innovation and entrepreneurship at the heart of what it does, you would expect to see this clearly articulated in its plan.

- See if there's evidence on the website or in the corporate plan that the university is investing in enterprise and employability initiatives for students and alumni.

- Look for evidence that the university's administration supports student entrepreneur societies and clubs.

- Check whether the university collaborates with external companies on enterprise projects and whether students can work on these projects.

- Check whether there is continued support before and after graduation with internship and alumni mentoring programmes.

v. Student participation: The level of student engagement and involvement in entrepreneurial activity can be a useful indicator of the success of the university's initiatives to promote enterprising thinking and entrepreneurial mind-sets.

 What to look out for when evaluating the level of student participation:

Factors indicative of a positive student engagement may include:

- Participation in enterprise activity from many academic disciplines and not only the business or management departments. For instance, teams competing in start-up competitions comprise of students from different academic disciplines;

- Enterprise programmes and workshops are open to and attended by the whole student base;

- Student teams feature consistently in national/international start-up competitions;

- Enterprising students are celebrated with awards and recognitions in a variety of competitions.

(d) External sources for assessing entrepreneurship

I appreciate that it may not always be easy to research university websites to assess their commitment to entrepreneurship. In this section, we shall consider external sources that could help you in your evaluation of entrepreneurship. These external sources identify areas of best practice and also highlight universities that have excelled in entrepreneurship. You can use these insights to evaluate your preferred universities and see how they measure up.

i. **The *Times Higher Education, Outstanding Entrepreneurial University Award:***

This award, sponsored by the National Centre for Entrepreneurship in Education (NCEE), is made annually in recognition of those universities that are excelling in embedding entrepreneurship. The award was known as the *Entrepreneurial University of the Year Award* (EUOTY).

To illustrate how certain universities have distinguished themselves in entrepreneurship, I have highlighted key achievements and activities of the top three finalists in *The Times Entrepreneurial University of the Year Award* (EUOTY) 2012 (Table 3). These achievements and activities give you an idea of best practice. As you are conducting your research, check if the universities you are considering have the same level of commitment to developing an entrepreneurial culture.

Table 3: Key Achievements of the Top 3 Finalists in the Entrepreneurial University of the Year Award (2012)

Finalists	Notable entrepreneurship achievements and activities
1. The University of Huddersfield	Enterprise is central to the institutional strategy in the form of two key strategic aims: (i) to produce employable and enterprising graduates; (ii) to contribute to economic, social and cultural development. Construction of an exemplar £12 million EU-funded cross-sector hub for open innovation.

Finalists	Notable entrepreneurship achievements and activities
	3M Buckley Innovation Centre, where global companies will sit alongside innovative start-ups and our best student and graduate businesses. Support for the best student businesses called *"Activ8 Your Business"* • Placement opportunities include working in entrepreneurial firms or starting your own business through the Enterprise Placement Year.
2. University of East Anglia (UEA)	Enterprise is a core element in the UEA Corporate Plan reflecting its place at the heart of our strategic agenda. UEA is part of the Norwich Research Park (NRP), contributing to the associated vibrant research and business community. Several university spin outs have offices in the NRP Innovation Centre, a hub of science and technology companies. Teams from UEA were supported in taking part in national & local competitions (winning the Biotech YES competition, taking second place in the FLUX competition and reaching the finals of the Npower Challenge).

Finalists	Notable entrepreneurship achievements and activities
	Students are funded to participate in the "i-teams" programme where they gain hands-on experience of investigating potential markets for new technology. £2m investment in Student Enterprise and Employability for students and alumni, and entrepreneurship professionals. Development of innovative courses such as the MA in Creative Entrepreneurship, supported by Barclays. Investment in building a new £15m purpose-built Enterprise Centre for students, staff, local businesses and entrepreneurs.
3. The University of Edinburgh	Edinburgh students have dominated Scottish business plan competitions. Student participation in the university's renowned "LAUNCH.ed" student enterprise programme. • Many first-time entrepreneurs return to LAUNCH.ed upon graduation for help with more substantial high-growth business propositions.

Source: The National Centre for Entrepreneurship in Education (NCEE)

You may find it useful to see which institutions have been recognised as excelling in entrepreneurship. Table 4 shows winners and finalists of the EUOTY award over the last ten years.

Table 4: Outstanding Entrepreneurial University Award - Winners and Finalists since 2008

Year	Winner	Finalists
2017/18	Liverpool John Moores University	• City University of London • Falmouth University • Pearson College London • University of Salford • Southampton Solent University
2016/17	London South Bank University	• Aston University • Coventry University • Manchester Metropolitan University • University of Central Lancashire • University of Lincoln
2015/16	University of Leeds	• University of Central Lancashire • University of Leeds • University of Lincoln • Loughborough University • Northumbria University • University of Nottingham

Year	Winner	Finalists
2014/15	Anglia Ruskin University	• Kingston University • Teesside University • University of Central Lancashire • University of Chester • University College London
2013/14	University of Strathclyde	• University of Chester • University of Lincoln • University of Sheffield • University of Surrey • Teesside University
2012/13	University of Huddersfield	• The University of Edinburgh • The University of Northampton • The University of East Anglia • The University of Huddersfield • The University of Strathclyde • Plymouth University
2011/12	Coventry University	• University of Central Lancashire • The University of Edinburgh • The University of Northampton • Plymouth University • The University of York

Year	Winner	Finalists
2010/11	University of Hertfordshire	• Brunel University • University of Central Lancashire • Imperial College London • University of Plymouth • Teesside University
2009/10	Queen's University Belfast	• Coventry University • University of Hertfordshire • University of Portsmouth • University of Surrey • University of Strathclyde
2008/09	University of Nottingham	• Coventry University • Queen's University Belfast • University of Leeds • University of Oxford • University of Salford

Source: The National Centre for Entrepreneurship in Education (NCEE)

ii. The UBI Global World Rankings of University-linked Business Incubators and Accelerators:

UBI Global is a European research initiative that aims to help business incubators around the world to be more competitive and efficient. Since 2013, UBI Global has published rankings of the performance of university-linked incubators identifying the leading incubation programs in the following categories:

- World Top Business Incubator – Managed by University

- World Top Business Incubator – Affiliated with University

- World Top Business Incubator – Collaborating with University

- World Top Business Accelerator – Linked to University

The top five performers in each category can be viewed on the website. Detailed reports are also available, if you provide basic personal information (e.g. name and email address). It should be noted that UBI Global benchmarks universities from across the world. As a result, you find that relatively few institutions per country make it to the final rankings.

It is a remarkable achievement for any institution to emerge in the top rankings of a world university benchmark exercise, so it is worth mentioning the UK incubator programmes have excelled in these rankings since 2013:

- The *SETsquared Partnership* achieved the top ranking in 2017/18 and 2015/16. SETsquared is a collaboration between the universities of Bath, Bristol, Exeter, Southampton and Surrey.

- The *Clarence Centre for Enterprise and Innovation* of London South Bank University was ranked 15th in 2017/18.

- The *Oxford Entrepreneurs Incubation Centre* of Oxford University was ranked 19th in 2013/14.

UBI Global rankings can be accessed through their website at *http://ubi-global.com/rankings/*.

Recap: Key points to remember when considering entrepreneurship:

What to look out for when researching university resources (including website, brochures):

- Entrepreneurship workshops: Check if the university offers training and workshops to encourage enterprise thinking.

- Start-up competitions and enterprise events: Look for evidence that the university hosts or supports these events.

- University-operated incubation centres: Check if the university has its own incubation centre and whether it is open to student projects.

- Organisational environment: Check for evidence that the university administration is committed to entrepreneurship (e.g. entrepreneurship is part of the strategic plan or mission).

- Student participation: Look for evidence of high levels of student engagement in entrepreneurial activity (e.g. teams from the university regularly participate in national/international business competitions).

External sources useful in gaining an understanding of best practices and to check which universities are excelling in promoting entrepreneurship:

- Times Higher Education, Outstanding Entrepreneurial University Award –
  http://ncee.org.uk/programmes/the-entrepreneurial-university/

- The UBI Global World Rankings of University-linked Business Incubators and Accelerator –
  http://ubi-global.com/rankings/

Graduate success story: Jianqiao (China)

 Jianqiao (China)

Jianqiao came to the UK as an international student from China. When she completed her studies in business and administration at Cranfield university, she undertook an internship at a leading UK bank. She then went on to work as a project manager for a German company. She is currently based in the UK where she continues to develop her career as a successful digital marketing consultant. In this section, she provides insights on her experience as an international student and provides advice for prospective and current students.

1. **Why did you decide to study in the UK?**

   I always wanted to study in an English country to broaden my experience. So, when I planned to study overseas, I looked at universities in the USA and the UK. Eventually, I chose the UK as it was more cost-effective and I felt that I had better chances in the admissions process.

2. **What factors influenced your choice of university?**

   University reputation and course ranking were important factors for me. At the time that I chose the university, I did not consider factors such as links to employers. With hindsight, I realise that factors such as a university's links with employers or employers can also be quite important.

3. **What influenced your decision to choose the course you took?**

   There are two main reasons I chose my course. Firstly, for financial reasons, as the course of study was recognised by my loan provider. I also felt I would benefit significantly from the modules available in my course.

4. Did your university experience match your expectations?

Yes, I was very satisfied with my university experience. I got the chance to study along with students from different countries. The intensity of the course really pushed my boundaries and I developed myself a lot through the course professionally and personally. I only wish that there would have been even more students from many other countries to make my experience more diverse.

5. Describe your job hunting experience in the UK.

As international students from China, it was very hard for us to look for a job in the UK. What really mattered in job hunting was how well you could sell your story in English in the UK.

If there is anything I would do differently, I would get my CV ready at the earliest opportunity. I would also keep brushing up my interview skills with help from classmates and the careers service.

6. What advice would you give to prospective students to help them make the most out of the university experience?

Study hard and play hard. Get out of your comfort zone. Get your CV ready as early as possible while brushing up on your interview skills.

Do not be afraid of making mistakes in front of your classmates and teachers because that is how you will learn. Talk to people and learn about yourself from the perspective of others so you can make progress day by day.

CHAPTER 3

Choosing the right course – it matters what subject you study

There are a variety of reasons students study particular subjects at university. Some students may choose subjects which they consider to be mandatory for certain vocations (e.g. a degree in engineering to become an engineer or medicine to become a doctor). Parental or family influence can also be a factor. Other factors include interest or academic curiosity in a particular subject and perceived career prospects.

International students surveyed for this book cited various reasons for the courses they studied, as outlined below:

 What former students say:

"My interest in the subject was the main influence for choosing law."
– **Niroshan (Sri Lanka)**

"I performed really well in my A-levels/foundation year and was advised to take on a finance course because I'd really excelled at economics and mathematics for economics. Then, I did not know much about Investment Banking because it wasn't an industry that had really developed back home by the time I was joining university. I was advised that it was the future." – **Angela (Uganda)**

"I chose my course because I felt it would help me gain essential skills and had a good reputation amongst employers." – **Adham (Lebanon)**

"The fact that I'd taken computer science at A level and I had been good at it. I wasn't interested in programming or engineering so the most sensible option available was to do a course that gave the technical knowledge at a high level but also gave the opportunity to apply that in a business perspective." – **Julie (Uganda)**

"The potential earnings associated with the qualification made it very attractive." – **Alok (India)**

"I knew I always wanted to be in the health sector but I wasn't sure in what capacity. Psychology was my first choice, and nutrition was my second. However, after a lot of counsel (mainly from my parents), I saw the importance of getting into a 'professional degree'" – **Nkatha (Kenya)**

The course you study at university will have a significant impact on your future career. Therefore, it is important for prospective students to gather as much information as possible about the career prospects linked to their intended course of study (e.g. the types of jobs or employers available for certain degree subjects).

Information about what students have actually done after graduating is useful for understanding the value of degree courses in the labour market. In this section, we shall consider what graduates in different subject areas have gone on to do after completing university.

We shall consider two key data sources for information about graduate destinations:

I.   The annual *What do graduates do? (WDGD)* report, which is useful to understand graduate outcomes in the short term (i.e. six months after graduation). The data in the 2017/18 WDGD report comes from HESA Destination of Leavers of Higher Education 2016/17 and analysis is by the Higher Education Careers Services Unit (HECSU).

II. The *Longitudinal Educational Outcomes (LEO)* report by the Department of Education. This report provides data on graduate outcomes in the long term (up to 10 years after graduation).

The insights from these reports and the data on career destinations linked to certain subjects will help prospective students to make informed decisions about what courses to study.

Top tip: Career prospects are important but should not be the only factor considered.

Career prospects are not the only factor to consider when choosing your degree subject. Your intended degree should be a subject you have a strong interest in and are likely to enjoy studying. Ideally, it should be aligned with subjects you are good at and thus likely to excel at.

There is no point choosing a subject you have no interest in simply because it has good prospects. It will only make your university experience miserable and increase the likelihood that you will drop out before completing your course.

Short term: how subjects, jobs and salaries compare

Every year, the Higher Education Statistics Agency (HESA) collects data on what UK and EU graduates are doing within six months of completing their courses using the Destinations of Leavers from Higher Education (DLHE) survey. The Higher Education Careers Services Unit (HECSU) and the Association of Graduate Careers Advisory Services (AGCAS) collaborate to analyse data from the DLHE surveys and produce an annual report entitled: *"What do graduates do?"* (WDGD).

The 2017/18 WDGD report has been used in this section to provide insights about graduate careers and the career prospects linked to different degree subjects. With over 248,000 graduates completing the DLHE survey, the WDGD report provides a comprehensive snapshot about what graduates go into as their first career destinations. Whilst the WDGD report and DLHE surveys provide valuable insights, they have some limitations that you need to know:

- The first job that a graduate accepts is not always indicative of their long-term career. The first job for many graduates might be temporary work to pay the bills while they continue to apply for other jobs. Examples of temporary work that graduates take on include retail, bars, and restaurant catering. Typically, the first six to twelve months after graduation is the time graduates will be most reliant on their degree. Factors such as work experience, industry knowledge, and personal networks become more important later in graduate careers.

- Although the WDGD covers many subjects, it does not include every subject. Many degree subjects and titles are grouped into broader categories. Notable subjects that are not covered in the WDGD report include medicine, dentistry and nursing.

- The DLHE survey is targeted at UK and EU domiciled graduates and may have limited relevance for international students, particularly those who have no intention of working in the UK after graduation. Nevertheless, the insights from the report are useful for understanding the career prospects for certain degree subjects. International students should also research their local home markets to find out what the prospects are for certain courses. In fact, certain UK courses may not even be recognised in their home countries.

- DLHE surveys do not explain why graduates chose their career paths or accepted a particular job.

- There may be other factors affecting trends in the data. For instance, macro-economic factors such as the slow-downs in the economy or financial crises could have an adverse impact on graduates in different employment sectors. For instance, students who graduated in 2008 entered the labour market at a very difficult time at the height of the financial crisis.

University Subjects and Career Destinations

Firstly, we shall look at the subjects available for undergraduate study and the career opportunities on offer based on the following subject groupings:

1. Business and administrative studies

2. Technology, engineering and maths

3. Humanities

4. Science

5. Social sciences

6. Creative arts

We shall also consider the various degree subjects included within these subject groupings and the career trends associated with these subjects based on the 2017/18 WDGD report.

1. *Business and Administrative Studies*

There are five major subjects included in this grouping: economics; finance and accountancy; business and management; marketing; and hospitality, leisure, tourism and transport.

Graduate outcomes and considerations for studying these subjects

Degrees relating to business and administrative studies are quite popular. Approximately 13.2% of all UK-domiciled undergraduates studied these subjects. From an employer's perspective, these subjects enable students to develop useful skills such as commercial acumen, initiative to solve problems and the ability to think strategically.

The WDGD report suggests that there are plenty of opportunities for graduates within this grouping. The percentage in full-time employment within six months of graduation ranges from 68.7% (Marketing) to 56.3% (Economics). These figures are positive considering the average percentage of graduates in full-time employment across all subjects is 54.8%. Graduates from this grouping can be found in many sectors such as financial services, consulting, fast-moving consumer goods and retail.

The percentage of graduates who pursue further studies is high, which may be reflective of fierce competition for graduate roles. Economics graduates in particular often require a master's degree or doctorate to secure economist roles. Many finance and accountancy roles require professional qualifications such as CIMA (Chartered Institute of Management Accountants) or ACCA (Association of Chartered Certified Accountants) – hence the need to undertake further studies.

Table 5 highlights the key outcomes for graduates in this grouping, six months after graduation.

Table 5: Graduate outcomes for the Business and Administrative
Studies grouping

Graduate Outcomes			
Percentage of graduates (1= highest; 5= Lowest)	In full-time employment	Unemployed	Further study
1	Marketing (68.7%)	Economics (6.7%)	Economics (14.5%)
2	Hospitality, Leisure, Tourism & Transport (62.9%)	Finance & Accountancy (6.7%)	Business & Management (9.7%)
3	Business & Management (62.5%)	Business & Management (6.1%)	Finance & Accountancy (8.6%)
4	Finance & Accountancy (59.4%)	Marketing (5.3%)	Hospitality, Leisure, Tourism & Transport (7.2%)
5	Economics (56.3%)	Hospitality, Leisure, Tourism & Transport (5%)	Marketing (6.1%)

Source: 2017/18 WDGD Report

Employment destinations

Economics – A significant proportion of graduates from Economics (59%) secured employment as business, human resources (HR) and finance professionals. Other leading areas where economics graduates secured employment included: marketing, public relations and sales professionals (9.5%); retail and catering (7.4%); clerical and secretarial (6.6%); and 4% fell into the catch-all category of "other occupations." Employers included the London Stock Exchange, UK Civil Service and the Scottish Government.

Finance and Accountancy – Most Finance and Accountancy graduates (54.3%) found employment as business, human resources (HR) and finance professionals. Additional key areas where they found employment included roles in: clerical, secretarial and numerical clerks (15.8%); retail and catering (7.4%); and other occupations (4.8%). Employers for these graduates included PwC, Santander, Forbes Watson, Audi, GE, and the Police.

Business and Management – A high proportion of graduates from Business and Management degrees found employment as business, human resources (HR) and finance professionals (24.5%) followed by roles in marketing, PR and sales (20.8%). Clerical, secretarial and numerical roles took 10.7% whilst retail and catering took 10.6%. Employers included Mulberry, House of Fraser, FDM, National Union of Students, and the Church of England.

Marketing – A high proportion of marketing graduates secured employment as marketing, PR and sales professionals (52.2%). Other notable employment destinations included: retail and catering (11.6%); business, HR and finance (8.9%); and other occupations (5.8%). Employers included Lidl, YMCA and media companies.

Hospitality, leisure, tourism and transport – Most graduates found employment as marketing, PR and sales professionals (28.1%). Graduates also obtained employment in retail and catering (16%); other occupations (14.8%); business, HR and finance (6.6%). Employers included the RAF, BAE Systems, as well as hotel and events companies.

Salaries

The average salary range of graduates in this grouping is quite broad and may vary depending on location of employment in the UK. Salaries for economics graduates range from £19,000 to £30,500. Finance and accountancy graduate salaries range from £18,600 to £27,400; whilst salaries with business and management graduates range from £17,400 to £25,700. Unfortunately, the WDGD report did not include salary data for graduates with degrees in marketing and hospitality, leisure, tourism and transport.

2. *Technology, Engineering and Mathematics*

There are six major subjects included in this grouping: computer science and IT; mathematics; architecture and building; civil engineering; electrical and electronic engineering and; mechanical engineering.

Graduate outcomes and considerations for studying these subjects

The WDGD report notes that graduates from this subject grouping contribute significantly to the UK economy (approximately 25% of the total economy and 50% of exports). The outlook is very positive for graduates with degrees in these subjects as there is enormous demand for these skills. It is estimated that 13 million new employees will be needed by 2024 to replace existing staff. There is also a significant shortage of engineering graduates, with employers reporting difficulty in filling their vacancies.

The high demand for graduates in this grouping is clear in the high percentage of graduates that secure full-time employment within six months of graduation. With the exception of mathematics, subjects within this grouping showed percentages of graduates in full-time employment ranging from 62.6% (computer science & IT) to 70.8% (architecture and building).

These figures are very positive considering the average percentage of graduates in full-time employment across all subjects is 54.8%. However, mathematics was the exception with 47.9% in full-time employment.

Table 6 highlights the key outcomes for graduates in this grouping, six months after graduation.

Table 6: Graduate outcomes for the Technology, Engineering and Mathematics grouping

Graduate Outcomes			
Percentage of graduates (1= highest; 5= Lowest)	In full-time employment	Unemployed	Further study
1	Architecture and building (70.8%)	Computer science and IT (9.8%)	Mathematics (23.4%)
2	Civil engineering (67.6%)	Electrical and electronic engineering (7.9%)	Civil engineering (14.3%)
3	Mechanical engineering (63.7%)	Mechanical engineering (7.6%)	Mechanical engineering (13.4%)
4	Electrical and electronic engineering (62.7%)	Mathematics (7.3%)	Computer science and IT (10.1%)
5	Computer science and IT (62.6%)	Civil engineering (5.4%)	Marketing (6.1%)
6	Mathematics (47.9%)	Architecture and building (5.3%)	Architecture and building (7.5%)

Source: 2017/18 WDGD Report

Employment destinations

Computer science and IT – A high proportion of graduates (61.5%) secured employment as IT professionals. Other key areas where computer science and IT graduates secured employment included retail and catering (8.6%); business, HR and finance (5.6%); and 5.5% fell into the catch-all category of "other occupations." Employers included IBM, Bloomberg, HP, Bank of America, RAF, EY, Tesco, Ocado, and Hilton.

Mathematics – A high proportion of mathematics graduates found employment as business, HR and finance professionals (41.3%) followed by roles in IT (12.6%); education (9.4%); took 10.7% whilst retail and catering (9.3%); Clerical, secretarial and numerical (7.3%); and other occupations (4.5%). Employers included Teach First, PwC, Deloitte, Goldman Sachs, Grant Thornton, NHS, and Matalan.

Architecture and building – Many graduates found employment as engineering and building professionals (46.8%); other professional and technical roles (25.8%); retail and catering (4.7%); and other occupations (3.8%). Employers included: NHS, Interserve, Network Rail, Thales, British Army, Morrisons, and Wetherspoons.

Civil engineering – A significant proportion secured employment as engineering and building professionals (72.6%); other professional and technical roles (5.3%); retail and catering (4.7%); and other occupations (4.5%). Employers included Amey, Shell, Aecom, Transport for London, Network rail, Lloyds, Barclays, PwC, Pendragon, Nandos, and Eddie Stobart.

Electrical and electronic engineering – Many graduates found employment as engineering and building professionals (40.6%); IT professionals (18.3%); retail and catering (7.8%); other professional and technical roles (6.4%); and other occupations (6.7%). Employers included Arup, National Grid, Rolls Royce, KPMG, JP Morgan, Jaguar Land Rover, Atkins, Siemens, and Superdrug.

Mechanical engineering – A significant percentage of graduates secured employment as engineering and building professionals (55.9%); other professional and technical roles (9.1%); retail and catering (6.4%); and other occupations (7.5%). Employers included Jaguar Land Rover, British Airways, Dyson, Nissan, Rolls Royce, Vodafone, RAF, Goldman Sachs, BAE, NHS, and Screwfix.

Salaries

The salary range for these subjects is wide and ranges from £18,000 to £30,000. Graduates in IT appear to achieve somewhat higher salaries at the top end; whereas architects get slightly lower salaries (which reflects the length of time spent at assistant level whilst they complete their professional portfolios).

3. *Humanities*

There are four major subjects included in this grouping: English, History, Languages and Philosophy.

Graduate outcomes and considerations for studying these subjects

Humanities are a traditional subject grouping that develops strong academic skills. Students usually study humanities courses for the enjoyment of the subject rather than for employability reasons. Therefore, they are more likely to develop their career plans alongside their studies.

Students may find it appealing that their employment options can be kept open, as humanities courses tend not to be restrictive about career prospects. The advantage of this career-openness is that humanities students could end up working in a varied range of jobs.

The down-side, though, is that graduates may take longer to progress into graduate careers than students who pursue degrees that are more vocationally-focused, due to prolonged exploration of career options. This may explain why the proportion of humanities graduates pursuing further studies is higher than other subjects. For instance, 26% of philosophy students and 23% of language graduates undertook further studies – considerably higher than the proportion across all subjects (15%).

It should be noted that the proportion of humanities graduates who are unemployed six months after graduation (history 6.1%, languages 6.5%, philosophy 6.0%, English 5.5%) is slightly higher than the average across all subjects (5%). Nevertheless, the wide range of occupations entered into by humanities graduates suggests that students develop transferable skills desirable for employers.

Table 7 highlights the key outcomes for graduates in this grouping, six months after graduation.

Table 7: Graduate outcomes for the Humanities grouping

Graduate Outcomes			
Percentage of graduates (1= highest; 5= Lowest)	In full-time employment	Unemployed	Further study
1	English (41.5%)	Languages (6.5%)	Philosophy (26.1%)
2	Philosophy (40.8%)	History (6.1%)	History (25.5%)
3	Languages (39.4%)	Philosophy (6.0%)	English (23.6%)
4	History (39.2%)	English (5.5%)	Languages (22.5%)

Source: 2017/18 WDGD Report

Employment destinations

English – The main employment destinations for English graduates are: retail and catering (17.9%); marketing, PR and sales (15.0%); clerical, secretarial and numerical (12.1%); and education (11.0%). Teaching is a popular aspiration with 28.2% pursuing post-graduate qualifications in education. Employers included British Army, Pfizer, Frontline, British Transport Police, CNN, Macmillan Publishing, NHS, and PureGym.

History – Notable career destinations for history graduates are: retail and catering (18.8%); business, HR and finance (13.5%); marketing, PR and sales (12.6%); clerical, secretarial and numerical (12.3%); other occupations (10.5%); and education (6.7.0%). Employers included KPMG, Nestle, HMRC, Science Museum Group, and NHS.

Languages – The main employment destinations for graduates are as follows: marketing, PR and sales (16.7%); business, HR and finance (13.5%); education (13.1%) retail and catering (12.7%); clerical, secretarial and numerical (12.7%); other occupations (6.9%). Teaching is a common destination with 21.6% undertaking further studies in education. Employers included PwC, British Council, NHS, BBC, Estee lauder, Amazon, and Lloyds Bank.

Philosophy – Notable career destinations for philosophy graduates include: business, HR and finance (16.5%); retail and catering (16.4%); marketing, PR and sales (13.0%); clerical, secretarial and numerical (9.7%); other occupations (9.1%); and education (6.8%). Employers included Lloyds Bank, Deloitte, and NHS.

Salaries

The range of salaries for humanities graduates is £15,000 to £26,000, with philosophy and history graduates having the highest earning potential.

4. *Science*

There are five major subjects included in this grouping: biology, chemistry, physical and geographical sciences, physics, and sports science.

Graduate outcomes and considerations
for studying these subjects

Although there is a range of opportunities available to science graduates, only a small proportion of graduates become science professionals within six months of graduation. This could be attributed to the relatively small number of science-focused employers plus the increased importance of post-graduate qualifications.

The outcome for chemistry graduates is positive with 17.9% becoming science professionals. The percentage of graduates who became science professionals was considerably lower for other science subjects – biology (9.9%), physics 6.8%, physical and geographical sciences 1.6%, and sports science 1.2%. Graduates from sports science gravitated towards careers as fitness instructors and sports coaching.

The skills developed from studying science courses are attractive to a wide range of employers, as evidenced by the proportion of graduates who commenced professional careers in non-science occupations. For instance, the percentage of graduates who became business, HR and finance professionals was 21.3% for physics, 14.9% for physical and geographical sciences, and 13.3% for chemistry.

A significant proportion of physics graduates (18.7%) opted for careers in IT. Science graduates were more likely to undertake further studies in comparison to graduates from other subjects.

Table 8 highlights the key outcomes for graduates in this grouping, six months after graduation.

Table 8: Graduate outcomes for the Science grouping

Graduate Outcomes			
Percentage of graduates (1= highest; 5= Lowest)	In full-time employment	Unemployed	Further study
1	Physical and geographical sciences (48.1%)	Physics (8.3%)	Physics (35.3%)
2	Sports science (44.5%)	Chemistry (6.7%)	Chemistry (33.2%)
3	Chemistry (43.0%)	Biology (6.3%)	Biology (32.5%)
4	Physics (38.7%)	Physical and geographical sciences (4.8%)	Physical and geographical sciences (21.7%)
5	Biology (35.6%)	Sports science (3.5%)	Sports science (21.0%)

Source: 2017/18 WDGD Report

Employment destinations

Biology – Notable career destinations for biology graduates six months after graduation are as follows: retail and catering (19.9%); other professional and technical roles (17.5%); science (9.9%); other occupations (9.3%); business, HR and finance (8.5%); clerical, secretarial and numerical (6.6%). Employers included Royal Navy, NHS, Virgin Media, L'Oreal, Bristol Zoo, and Ministry of Defence.

Chemistry – The main employment destinations for graduates are as follows: other professional and technical roles (19.6%); science 17.9%); business, HR and finance (13.3%); retail and catering (10.6%); other occupations (5.6%). Employers included Network Rail, Tata steel, Deloitte, Royal Society of Chemistry, Unilever, and the Police.

Physical and geographical sciences – Career destinations for graduates are as follows: retail and catering (17.4%); other professional and technical roles (16.0%); business, HR and finance (14.9%); other occupations (9.6%); clerical, secretarial and numerical (8.3%). Employers included: Royal Air Force, AECOM, Samsung, and Glasgow Airport.

Physics – Notable career destinations for graduates six months after graduation are as follows: business, HR and finance (21.3%); IT (18.7%); retail and catering (9.7%); engineering and building (7.8%); education (7.6%); science (6.8%); other professional and technical roles (6.4%); other occupations (5.7%). Employers included NHS, BAE Systems, Experian, Royal Navy, Amazon, and Starbucks.

Sports science – Career destinations for graduates include: other professional and technical roles (24.7%); retail and catering (14.3%); other occupations (12.2%); education (7.6%) business, HR and finance (5.6%). Teaching is a popular destination for graduates with 31.5% undertaking a post-graduate qualification in education. Employers included Scottish Ambulance Service, Barclays, RBS, bet365, and British Airways.

Salaries

The salary scale is quite broad and ranges from £17,000 to £29,000. Physics graduates are on the higher end (£18,500 - £29,000), followed by chemistry (£18,200 - £26,600). Biology was at the lower end (£17,000-£22,800).

5. *Social sciences*

There are five major subjects included in this grouping: geography, law, psychology, sociology, and politics.

Graduate outcomes and considerations for studying these subjects

Social science graduates rarely favour a specific vocational outcome and progress into a wide variety of occupations. The only exception to this is law, where most graduates pursue careers in the legal sector. Sociology and psychology graduates preferred roles that were closely related to their subject of study (e.g. legal, social and welfare occupations).

Many social science graduates pursued further studies, in broadly similar proportions to humanities graduates. A significant proportion of law graduates undertook further studies (30.8%). This is not surprising given an undergraduate degree alone is not sufficient to enter legal practice. Law graduates would have to complete the Legal Practice Course or Bar Professional Training Course before embarking on a legal career.

Psychology graduates were also highly likely to undertake further studies (20.7%), which may reflect the need to gain post-graduate qualifications to go into healthcare roles.

Within this group, graduates from politics and sociology were more likely to be unemployed at 6.7% and 6.1% respectively.

The key outcomes for graduates in this grouping six months after graduation are outlined in table 9.

Table 9: Graduate outcomes for the Social Sciences grouping

Graduate Outcomes			
Percentage of graduates (1= highest; 5= Lowest)	In full-time employment	Unemployed	Further study
1	Sociology (46.6%)	Politics (6.7%)	Law (30.8%)
2	Geography (46.2%)	Sociology (6.1%)	Psychology (20.7%)
3	Politics (45.0%)	Geography (5.7%)	Politics (23.3%)
4	Psychology (41.7%)	Psychology (5.0%)	Geography (21.4%)
5	Law (39.4%)	Law (4.9%)	Sociology (18.2%)

Source: 2017/18 WDGD Report

Employment destinations

Geography – The main employment destinations for graduates are as follows: business, HR and finance (21.7%); retail and catering (15.1%); marketing, PR and sales (13.0%); clerical secretarial and numerical (8.4%); other occupations (7.2%). Employers included Lloyds Banking, Qatar Airways, Frontline, Enterprise Rent-a-Car, Stirling Council, and Costa.

Law – Career destinations for graduates are as follows: legal, social and welfare (33.8%); retail and catering (13.9%); clerical secretarial and numerical (12.3%); business, HR and finance (12.0%); other occupations (6.9%). Employers included Proctor & Gamble, Teach First, HMRC, Deloitte, Citizens Advice Bureau, Civil Service, Brattle Group, HM Court Service, and Next.

Psychology – Notable career destinations for graduates six months after graduation are as follows: childcare, health and education (16.2%); legal, social and welfare (14.0%); retail and catering (15.8%); clerical secretarial and numerical (10.2%); business, HR and finance (8.4%); other occupations (7.5%). Employers included Majestic Wines, University of Central Lancashire, Frontline, HSBC, KPMG, Connells, and Marks & Spencer.

Sociology – Career destinations for graduates include: retail and catering (20.2%); clerical secretarial and numerical (12.4%); legal, social and welfare (12.2%); other occupations (11.2%); business, HR and finance (9.4%); childcare, health and education (8.8%). Employers included Priory Group, American Express, Milton Keynes College, Walmart, and Knight Frank.

Politics – Career destinations for graduates are as follows: business, HR and finance (20.3%); marketing, PR and sales (16.9%); retail and catering (13.4%); clerical secretarial and numerical (9.7%) other occupations (8.3%). Employers included Waitrose, Aviva, CBS UK, Scottish Parliament, British army, O2, and Price Forbes.

Salaries

The range of salaries for social science graduates is £15,900 to £25,900.

6. *Creative arts*

There are four major subjects included in this grouping: fine arts, design, media studies, and performing arts.

Graduate outcomes and considerations for studying these subjects

Graduates from creative subjects find employment in a wide range of sectors. The emergence of digital and social media has created a wealth of opportunities that are well suited to graduates from the creative arts. It is estimated that the UK creative industry is growing four times faster than the workforce as a whole according to the Department for Digital, Culture, Media and Sport.

Portfolio careers are more commonplace for graduates in creative arts. This means that graduates in creative arts are more likely to have more than one role in multiple locations, which altogether make up a full-time wage.

It is no wonder that the percentage of graduates from this grouping who indicated that they were self-employed or working freelance was remarkably higher than other subjects. For instance, the percentage for fine arts was 17.8%, performing arts 23.3%, and designs 12.2% – which was much higher when compared to the figure from the general student population (4.6%). With high levels of freelance work, graduates need to be more proactive and resilient to create employment opportunities.

The figures of graduates pursuing further studies are generally lower in comparison to graduates from other subjects. Graduates from performing arts are more likely to pursue teaching qualifications than the other subjects in the creative arts grouping.

The key outcomes for graduates in this grouping six months after graduation are outlined in the table 10.

Table 10: Graduate outcomes for the Creative Arts grouping

Graduate Outcomes			
Percentage of graduates (1= highest; 5= Lowest)	In full-time employment	Unemployed	Further study
1	Design (57.6%)	Media studies (8.8%)	Fine arts (14.9%)
2	Media studies (49.3%)	Fine arts (6.9%)	Performing arts (14.5%)
3	Performing arts (42.1%)	Design (5.8%)	Media studies (9.9%)
4	Fine arts (38.3%)	Performing arts (5.4%)	Design (5.8%)

Source: 2017/18 WDGD Report

Employment destinations

Fine arts – Career destinations for graduates are as follows: arts, design and media (27.7%); retail and catering (26.5%); other occupations (12.0%); childcare, health and education (5.8%); clerical secretarial and numerical (5.8%); marketing, PR and sales (5.2%). Employers included Lloyds Banking, Jobcentre Plus, and Impact Arts.

Design – The main employment destinations for graduates are as follows: arts, design and media (43.9%); retail and catering (18.0%); marketing, PR and sales (9.5%); other occupations (8.5%). Employers included Marks & Spencer, Leeds Building Society, Wren Kitchens, Amarelle, and National Museum of Scotland.

Media studies – Career destinations for graduates include: retail and catering (24.5%); arts, design and media (22.7%); marketing,

PR and sales (16.0%); other occupations (10.9%); clerical secretarial and numerical (7.2%). Employers included Apple, Sky Media, Newsdirect Wales, and American Diner.

Performing arts – Career destinations for graduates are as follows: arts, design and media (31.6%); retail and catering (20.3%); other occupations (10.7%); education (8.1%); clerical secretarial and numerical (6.0%); marketing, PR and sales (5.9%); childcare, health and education (5.1%). Employers included John Lewis, Saffery Champness, Wales Millennium Centre, and TUI.

Salaries

Annual salaries for creative arts graduates range from £14,000 to £22,900.

Long term: how subjects, jobs and salaries compare

The LEO report is another useful information source for understanding graduate destinations. It is published by the Department of Education and provides salary and outcomes information on UK domiciled graduates. It helps us to understand how much graduates from different UK universities studying different courses earn over a longer time horizon (up to 10 years after graduation). This is done by aggregating a lot of useful data such as salary, benefits, tax and student loans from government bodies such as *Her Majesty's Revenue and Customs* and the *Department for Work and Pensions*.

The LEO's fifth release was published in March 2018. For the first time, it includes an assessment of graduate outcomes based on whether the graduate was domiciled in the UK or EU or from an overseas country, prior to study. Therefore, it is a useful data source in relation to graduate outcomes for international students.

Whilst the LEO report provides useful data and insights, it has some limitations which should be noted. Firstly, LEO information is not all-inclusive. For instance, certain institutions will have high proportions of graduates with *"activity not recorded."*

Additionally, the LEO report should not be viewed as an indicator of performance or the sole basis for predicting future earnings. It is historical data, and there are so many other variables that affect the jobs market (e.g. the state of the economy). Therefore, too much reliance should not be placed on past outcomes as a predictor of future earnings.

Despite these limitations, the LEO data is useful for understanding graduate outcomes. As the 2018 report includes data on UK, EU and overseas students, it has significant relevance for international students. We shall now consider the 2018 LEO report to draw out the key points.

Highlights from the 2018 LEO report

i. Earnings by subject studied

The data shows that graduates from Medicine & Dentistry have the highest earnings, whilst graduates from creative arts & design have the lowest earnings. Annual salary increases can also vary significantly depending on the subject. For instance, over a ten-year period, median earnings for economics graduates increased by £23,500; whereas median salaries for English studies increased by £11,600.

Table 11: Median Earnings by subject studied one, three, five and ten years after graduation

Subject	Years after Graduation			
	One	Three	Five	Ten
Medicine & Dentistry	£36,000	£42,800	£47,300	£55,100
Subjects Allied to Medicine (excluding Nursing)	£21,000	£24,400	£26,400	£29,600
Nursing	£25,500	£27,200	£28,500	£30,300
Biological Sciences (excluding Psychology)	£16,200	£21,100	£24,500	£30,700
Psychology	£16,300	£20,100	£22,600	£26,700
Veterinary Science	£28,300	£32,400	£34,900	£36,000
Agriculture and related subjects	£16,500	£19,100	£20,500	£24,300
Physical Sciences	£19,600	£23,800	£27,100	£32,800
Mathematical Sciences	£22,500	£28,000	£33,100	£40,300
Computer Science	£21,100	£25,200	£27,800	£34,200

Subject	Years after Graduation			
	One	Three	Five	Ten
Engineering & Technology	£25,100	£29,500	£32,600	£40,000
Architecture, Building & Planning	£23,200	£28,600	£30,900	£36,600
Social Studies (excluding Economics)	£18,000	£21,800	£24,500	£28,900
Economics	£24,500	£31,500	£37,900	£48,000
Business & Administrative Studies	£19,400	£23,400	£26,800	£32,200
Mass Communications & Documentation	£15,900	£19,700	£22,800	£27,300
Languages (excluding English Studies)	£19,300	£24,100	£27,400	£31,000
English Studies	£16,300	£21,400	£24,000	£27,900
Historical & Philosophical Studies	£17,400	£22,200	£25,400	£29,300
Creative Arts & Design	£14,300	£17,800	£20,200	£23,200
Education	£18,300	£21,600	£23,700	£27,500

Source: Department of Education

ii. Employment and salary outcomes based on mode of study

The LEO shows outcomes for graduates based on their mode of study, i.e., part-time, full-time, and sandwich courses (i.e., degrees with an industry placement).

The data shows favourable outcomes for graduates from sandwich courses as they earn more and are also more likely to be in sustained employment or further study. This underscores the advantage sandwich course students who enter the graduate market, having already gained experience from their industry placement.

Table 12: Employment outcomes and salaries based on mode of study

[Key: (%) indicates the percentage of graduates in further study, sustained employment or both; and (£) indicates the median earnings].

Study Mode	Years after graduation							
	One		Three		Five		Ten	
	%	£	%	£	%	£	%	£
Full-time	86.3	18,200	86.6	22,200	85.6	24,300	83.0	30,200
Sandwich	87.2	23,200	88.1	27,900	86.3	31,300	83.1	36,400
Part-time	86.2	22,800	85.1	24,700	83.8	25,900	79.6	29,300

Source: Department of Education

In the table 12; **(%)** indicates the percentage of graduates in further study, sustained employment or both; and **(£)** indicates the median earnings.

iii. The significance of prior attainment

Prior attainment refers to the performance of students before university. Usually, this will be based on the qualification and points gained before undertaking undergraduate study.

The LEO report shows that graduates' salary potential can be linked to prior attainment, and prior attainment can be significant to graduates' salary potential and earnings.

As indicated in table 13, the proportion of graduates in sustained employment, further study or both can be directly linked to prior attainment. The data also shows that graduates with higher prior attainment were more likely to start their careers with higher median earnings. Additionally, graduates with higher prior attainment were more likely to achieve significant annual salary increases. For instance, graduates with "AAAA or above" gained an increase of £11,500 over five years; whereas graduates with "BTECs" gained £5,500 over the same period.

Table 13: Employment outcomes and median salaries linked to prior attainment

[Key: (%) indicates the percentage of graduates in further study, sustained employment or both; and (£) indicates the median earnings].

Prior attainment band	Years after graduation					
	One		Three		Five	
	%	£	%	£	%	£
AAAA or above	88.1	27,900	89.2	33,600	86.2	39,400
360 points	87.0	23,500	88.4	29,200	87.2	33,900
300-359 points	87.0	19,600	87.9	24,700	87.1	28,500

| Prior attainment band | Years after graduation | | | | | |
| | One | | Three | | Five | |
	%	£	%	£	%	£
240-299 points	86.9	18,100	87.9	22,500	86.9	25,800
Below 240 points	86.5	17,200	87.5	21,000	87.2	24,000
1 or 2 A level passes	84.9	17,000	86.3	20,700	85.6	22,700
BTEC	85.7	15,900	86.6	19,000	86.8	21,400
Other	85.5	16,900	85.8	20,300	85.2	23,500

Source: Department of Education

iv. Earnings for overseas domiciled graduates by subject

The LEO report includes data on salaries for overseas domiciled graduates over a five-year period. Overseas domiciled graduates would include international students who graduated in the UK and took up employment in the UK. Salaries for UK and EU domiciled graduates are also included allowing for comparison of earnings for different subjects as shown in table 14.

Table 14: Earnings five years after graduation by subject and domicile

Subject	Annualised earnings by domicile (five years after graduation)		
	Overseas	UK	EU
Medicine & Dentistry	£48,200	£47,300	£45,500
Subjects Allied to Medicine (excluding Nursing)	£31,200	£26,400	£29,400
Nursing	£25,500	£28,500	£30,200
Biological Sciences (excluding Psychology)	£26,200	£24,500	£28,100
Psychology	£27,000	£22,600	£24,100
Veterinary Science	-	£34,900	-
Agriculture and related subjects	£21,700	£20,500	£26,200
Physical Sciences	£29,100	£27,100	£29,200
Mathematical Sciences	£48,600	£33,100	£37,600
Computer Science	£26,400	£27,800	£37,800
Engineering & Technology	£32,600	£32,600	£33,500
Architecture, Building & Planning	£28,800	£30,900	£28,300
Social Studies (excluding Economics)	£26,000	£24,500	£27,900
Economics	£45,700	£37,900	£41,700

Subject	Annualised earnings by domicile (five years after graduation)		
	Overseas	UK	EU
Law	£28,500	£25,200	£34,200
Business & Administrative Studies	£23,800	£26,800	£30,000
Mass Communications & Documentation	£25,000	£22,800	£25,300
Languages (excluding English Studies)	£25,500	£27,400	£28,400
English Studies	£24,700	£24,000	£23,700
Historical & Philosophical Studies	£29,200	£25,400	£26,500
Creative Arts & Design	£23,700	£20,200	£19,500
Education	£24,300	£23,700	£22,100

Source: Department of Education

The data shows that subjects with the most variability in earnings between different domiciles included: Mathematical Sciences (Overseas: £48,600, UK: £33,100, EU: £37,600) and Computer Science (Overseas: £26,400, UK: £27,800, EU: £37,800). Whereas the subjects with the least variability in earnings between different domiciles included: Physical Sciences (Overseas: £29,100, UK: £27,100, EU: £29,200); Engineering & Technology (Overseas: £32,600, UK: £32,600, EU: £33,500); and English Studies (Overseas: £24,700, UK: £24,000, EU: £23,700).

Recap: Main points to remember from the LEO data

1. **Salary and earnings can vary significantly based on subject studied**

   The data shows that there are significant differences in earnings based on subject studied with some subjects at the high end of earning potential (medicine and dentistry) and others at the low end of the salary scale (creative arts).

   Additionally, salary increments vary significantly depending on the subject. For instance, over a ten-year period, median earnings for economics graduates increased by £23,500, whereas median salaries for English studies increased by £11,600.

2. **Sandwich courses enhance employment outcomes**

   The data shows that favourable outcomes for graduates from sandwich courses as they have higher earning potential and are also more likely to be in sustained employment or further study.

3. **Prior attainment is important to employment outcomes**

   Academic performance and qualifications before university can impact your earning potential in the long term.

Other important factors to consider when choosing courses

Following the consideration of data about career outcomes considered above, there are additional factors that international students need to consider when choosing their courses. These factors are relevant because of differences in labour markets around the world.

These differences can have an impact on international students as they will achieve UK qualifications for careers in their home countries (or elsewhere around the world). In particular, students may not realise that not every UK qualification or course of study has equivalence in their home country.

For instance, an accounting qualification from the UK may not directly apply to practice as an accountant in a different country. Outlined below are top tips for students to consider when choosing their university courses.

 Top tips for international students when choosing courses

1. **Professional qualifications:**

   If you are interested in pursuing specific professional vocations in your home country (e.g. medicine, law, engineering), check that the UK degree course you're interested in will be recognised by the relevant professional body or regulatory authority in your home country.

   Most countries have their own local requirements about the minimum qualifications required to practice in certain professions. For instance, admission into legal practice in many jurisdictions will require successful completion of a post-graduate legal qualification (often referred to as "Law School"). Typically, most law schools will specify entry level requirements including: (i) whether UK undergraduate degrees are recognised; (ii) whether there are mandatory modules that must be completed as part of your undergraduate degree.

   Doing this research before you commit to a particular degree course will ensure that you do not face any restrictions if you pursue certain professional vocations in your home country after you complete your studies in the UK.

2. **Specialised subjects:**

   Given the highly competitive labour market, it may be appealing for prospective students to enrol for niche degree courses hoping that this will give them an advantage when applying for jobs. However, pursuing niche undergraduate courses can be a risky strategy as it could also restrict job opportunities very early in your career.

   For instance, if you were considering a career in finance with a focus on investments and securities, you choose a specialised degree in investments and securities. However, this may limit the jobs you could apply for as not every financial company has an investments and securities business. Recruiters may disregard your job application because your area of specialisation is not relevant for them. If you opt for a degree that is not considered too specialised, you will have more job opportunities to apply for.

   If you have a strong interest in certain subjects, it would be better to opt for a generalised degree that has electives or modules with those specialist subjects (e.g. a finance degree with modules on investments and securities).

3. **Recognised degree subjects:**

   Be mindful about choosing courses which could be perceived as irrelevant or not as intellectually rigorous as traditional subjects. There are many new degree subjects that look appealing to students but would not be recognised by future employers. In the UK, such courses have been dubbed "Mickey Mouse degrees" because they are considered worthless.

4. **Relevance to your home country:**

   Prospective students should also consider the relevance of their degree course to the labour market in their home countries. For instance, you may choose a course about the oil and gas industry but your home country has no such industry.

Therefore, you run the risk that your degree will have limited applicability to that labour market. When considering your degree subjects, ask yourself whether there is a thriving industry or job market where your degree subject would be applicable.

5. **Integrated Masters Degrees:**

Integrated Masters degrees start as a Bachelor's degree but continue for an extra year, conferring a Master's degree on completion. For this reason, integrated Masters programmes can be very attractive to international students.

Integrated Masters programmes feature in certain university systems and can be advantageous for certain careers (e.g. where further study meets professional requirements).

If students are attracted to integrated programmes because they want to attain a Master qualification, they should carefully weigh the advantages and disadvantages. Some questions students could consider before committing to an integrated programme are as follows:

(a). Would it be more advantageous to attain a Master's qualification at a different institution (perhaps one that is more highly rated in terms of teaching, research, etc.)?

(b). Would it be more cost effective to undertake a Master's degree at a different institution?

(c). Would you be prepared to commit to a particular Masters programme before you have started the undergraduate degree? What if your career goals change midway through your undergraduate degree;

would you be willing to continue for an extra year knowing you want to pursue a different career?

(d). Will an integrated programme at the same institution and location in the UK give you the student experience you desire? Perhaps you would prefer to pursue a Master's programme in a different city to broaden your experience of living in the UK.

 Useful information and resources

Online resources and books with guidance about applying for university.

- *"University Degree Course Offers,"* Brian Heap.

- Heap Online - *http://www.heaponline.co.uk/*

- Universities and Colleges Admissions Service (UCAS) - *https://www.ucas.com/*

Graduate success story: Edward (Ghana)

 Edward (Ghana)

Edward came to the UK as an international student from Ghana. He studied Business Administration at Cardiff University. On graduating he worked for the Royal Bank of Scotland for two years before pursuing further studies at Cornell University in the US. Edward is now based in Ghana where he has developed a successful career in public service, first as a Technical Consultant and currently as the Principal Economics Officer for the Ministry of Finance.

1. Why did you decide to study in the UK?

There were two main reasons, i.e., both push and pull factors. The main push factor was what I perceived as falling academic standards in Ghana and deterioration in infrastructural facilities on campus. I was actually admitted to a prestigious local university, which recruited top performing A level students.

However, during orientation I realised that the university had significant resource challenges which would have a negative impact on my university experience. During this same period, there were severe disruptions in the academic calendar resulting in lecture strikes and government policy disruptions. I subsequently concluded that the time was now to challenge myself by seeking opportunities overseas.

The pull factor was the attraction of going to pursue a degree programme in a new and foreign environment. Although foreign, it was comfortable enough because of the language similarities. I found this very appealing, so the UK was a natural fit for a young gentleman like me coming from Ghana.

2. What factors influenced your choice of university?

The main factor was the ranking of the school for the programme of study that I was interested in pursuing. Other minor considerations included size of the city (i.e., not too big or too small) and proximity to London.

3. What influenced your decision to choose the course you took?

Based on my high school programme of study and also the marketability of the programme in question both in Ghana and internationally.

4. Did your university experience match your expectations?

Yes, it did. Cardiff University was a top-quality university with good lecturers and also solid internship opportunities for practical training.

5. Describe your job hunting experience in the UK.

I found job hunting more difficult than I had expected both in terms of applying for internships/placements as well as full-time graduate roles. I think that the main reasons were cultural adaptation, work permit status and the need to fit into the system. I found that some of the knowledge that I had gained from my studies were useful during the interview and assessment centre stages of the recruitment process.

If there was anything I would do differently, in relation to job applications, I would try and be more assertive during the assessment centre. The Ghanaian, in me which is about harmony and accommodation based on minimal friction, was seen as being passive and unassertive.

6. **What advice would you give to prospective students to help them make the most of the university experience?**

- Always aim to select a university which is at the cutting edge of research and tuition in your area of choice.

- Be more socially active, join useful student organisations (e.g. debating clubs or writing clubs). It will help you to adapt culturally.

- When applying for jobs, always spread your options across your industry of choice based on size and relevance. For example, you are interested in an accounting career, apply to the "Big 4" accounting firms as well as other small boutique firms.

PART TWO

While at university

CHAPTER 4

First year

"Never underestimate the power you have to take your life in a new direction."
– Germany Kent

"Every moment is a fresh beginning."
– T.S. Eliot

New beginnings

Starting your university experience as an international student is truly exciting. Although many years and life events have occurred since my time as a fresh undergraduate, I can vividly recall the thrill of starting a new chapter of my life in a new country.

Hopefully, you will feel just as excited as you realise that unlimited possibilities lie before you. You have worked hard to get into university and have come a long way to make it happen. Don't worry if you also feel a bit anxious, especially as you think about friends and family you've left behind.

Every new adventure will feel somewhat daunting but fix your mind on the incredible opportunities that lie ahead – new friendships and new experiences. Whatever dreams or ambitions you aspire to, embrace the opportunity you now have to make them a reality.

If you are reading this chapter before "Freshers' Week," I commend you for your diligence. However, you ought to enjoy every opportunity as you start university so please put this book down, go out, socialise, make friends and have a great time. You can resume reading this after Fresher's Week and we can get back to the serious business of career planning.

Culture shock

Most international students, particularly those who have never lived abroad, will experience some form of culture shock during their first few months of arriving in the UK. Culture shock refers to the emotional or psychological experience a person may have when they move from a cultural environment they are familiar with to a foreign one.

It is the shock of having to adapt to a new environment, learning new ways of living, learning a new language, etc. It also includes the impact of missing the familiar and being separated from family and friends.

It is important for international students to understand when they are experiencing the effects of culture shock so that they can manage them. Students cope differently to culture shock and most students generally adapt well. However, some students never fully adjust to living in the UK.

Unfortunately, this can often have an adverse impact on their entire student experience, including their academic performance and career prospects on completing university. Having experienced culture shock myself and recalling the negative experiences of some students who eventually had to drop out, I think it is useful to cover this in some detail in this section.

Having this awareness will help you manage your way through the various stages of the culture shock cycle. It may also enable you to help others who may be experiencing culture shock.

Causes of culture shock

Some of the main elements contributing to culture shock for international students include:

- Weather: Many international students will find the UK weather depressing. Those who have never experienced winter or cold climates will find it even more difficult to adapt to. The long nights and short days of winter can feel unbearable, too, and have a negative effect on your mood. If it is any consolation, many UK residents also struggle to cope with the weather.

- Language: If English is not your first language, you may find it tiring to communicate in English all the time. Even if you are fluent in English, you are likely to experience different regional accents that can make communication a bit frustrating.

- Social norms: All cultures have codes or rules which affect the way they behave. Unfortunately, some of these codes are unspoken and not obvious, which can be very confusing for international students. Don't worry, you will learn these unwritten codes gradually – e.g. don't jump queues and stand on the right side of the escalator (walk on the left). The British generally have a reputation for punctuality. In business and academic life, keeping to time is important. Ensure that you are always on time for classes, meetings and appointments.

- Food: You may miss a familiar cuisine and find British food is not to your taste. If you are struggling to adjust to British cuisine, you could try and find suppliers of familiar food near your university. At universities where there are large communities of people from your country, you are likely to find a supplier for your local cuisine. I recall from my university days that there were local suppliers with thriving businesses that delivered home-made food at student-friendly prices.

Phases of culture shock

There are various models that help explain culture shock. Figure 1 illustrates the key phases of culture shock that international students are likely to experience.

Figure 1: The phases of culture shock

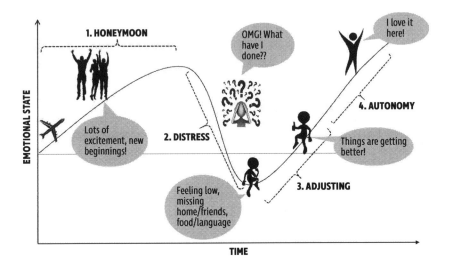

- Honeymoon phase – This describes the phase when you have first arrived, when you are excited about new beginnings. Almost everything about your new environment is exciting and you are intrigued about the differences in culture.

- Distress phase – During this phase, you may start to feel overwhelmed, isolated, or confused by the different cultural environment. You also feel that you do not have the familiar support network of family and friends. You may also feel frustrated or even hostile to the new cultural environment.

- Adjusting phase – In this phase, you start to accept differences and similarities. You become a bit more relaxed and confident as your new environment starts to feel more familiar. You're feeling better able to cope with different situations based on your growing experience.

- Autonomy phase – In this phase, your confidence increases significantly that you feel comfortable in your new environment and able to participate fully in the new host culture.

How to manage culture shock

It is important to recognise culture shock so you can manage it and prevent it from having an adverse impact on your university experience. Here are a few tips on managing culture shock:

- Firstly, acknowledge that it is a perfectly normal experience to go through culture shock. It does not mean that there is anything wrong with you.

- Maintain regular contact with family and friends in your home country. Fortunately, technology now affords students more options, so take advantage of the channels available (e.g. Skype, FaceTime, WhatsApp) and stay connected.

- Take advantage of any orientation programmes run by the university, particularly during the first couple of weeks after you start. These programmes can be very useful in helping you build a support network and finding other useful sources of information.

- Socialise and make friends with other international students (from your home country or other cultures). You will find these networks very encouraging and supportive as you will all probably be experiencing similar challenges. Also make friends with the local students so that you can adapt more quickly to your new environment.

- Regular exercise will keep you healthy and enhance your overall wellbeing.

- Try and find a supplier of familiar food, if possible. Ask other students from your home country who have been around longer as they may have already found suppliers. Also, student societies may be a good source of information for where you can find suppliers.

- If faith is important to you, find a local place of worship at the university or nearby where you can attend.

- Do not let yourself become isolated; you're not alone in what you are going through. Find a friend or someone to talk to if you feel you are struggling to cope or feeling unsettled. There are campus services or people at the university you can contact such as International Student Advisers, Counselling and Wellbeing services, or your Personal Tutor.

Useful information and resources

- Online resource that prepares students for cultural transition. Although designed for US students, it is applicable to international students generally: *https://www2.pacific.edu/sis/culture/*

- Elefriends is a safe place to listen, share and be heard: *https://www.elefriends.org.uk/*

- If you are feeling depressed, **Students against Depression** is a website by students for students. It offers advice, guidance and resources suited to the experiences of students: *https://www.studentsagainstdepression.org/*

- **HOST** is an organisation that links international students with friendly approved hosts who offer an invitation to their home for a day, weekend, or at Christmas: *http://www.hostuk.org/*

- **UK Council for International Student Affairs** (UKCISA) is the UK's national advisory body serving the interests of international students. You can find guidance on dealing with culture shock: *https://www.ukcisa.org.uk/Information--Advice/Preparation-and-Arrival/Facing-culture-shock*

- **Headspace** is a meditation app, helping users to manage stress, focus more and even sleep better: *https://www.headspace.com/headspace-meditation-app*

- The CMHA provides various services on mental health and wellbeing for Chinese people in the UK: *http://www.cmha.org.uk/*

Remember, culture shock is a normal experience and not a sign that you cannot adapt to your new environment. You should treat the experience as an important learning opportunity, helping you to become versatile and adaptable to change. The experience will equip you with valuable life skills and is one of the benefits of studying abroad.

Managing culture shock can also demonstrate to future employers that you are a resilient individual able to adapt well to a different cultural environment. You may even find that later on in life, you will have many interesting stories to share from your experiences.

Laying the foundations for career development

By this time, the term will have commenced, and hopefully, you will be more familiar with the university environment. Fresher's week may start to feel like a distant (but happy) memory, and you are getting into the whole university routine with lectures, tutorials, socialising etc.

As you get into the swing of your first year, you will need to start planning and charting out certain activities to ensure your career plan is on the right track. Many students don't realise that the academic year is shorter than it seems.

If you are not proactive in seeking out opportunities to further your career development, you may find yourself at a disadvantage. In this section, we shall cover the key activities you should be undertaking in your first year.

1. Get involved in co-curricular activities

In addition to gaining an academic qualification, university also provides wonderful opportunities to become involved in lots of interesting co-curricular activities. These activities may include a wide variety of sports, hobbies or even charity-based ventures. Participating in co-curricular activities will help you enjoy the university experience and help you build your networks, whilst having fun.

Getting involved in co-curricular activities is also very advantageous for your career development, as it provides the opportunity to develop many competencies that will be useful for future careers. These competencies include: effective communication, teamwork, planning, taking initiative, etc. Later on, as you apply for internships or graduate roles, you can then draw on your involvement in various co-curricular activities to showcase your abilities.

During your first year, research the university clubs or societies you think you will find interesting. There is no shortage of the weird and wonderful in clubs and societies. Some of these will be a laugh but may not have any value on your CV.

I would advise you to consider societies that are quite active throughout the year. Narrow down your selection to one or two societies where you can become actively involved and even take responsibility for some activities. Such involvement will make you an invaluable part of the university community, whilst also enhancing your career development.

2. Visit the university Careers Service

Find out about the upcoming events – Visit the university Careers Service or Employability Unit and get an overview of their services, key activities for the year, and events on the calendar (e.g. employability workshops, recruitment fairs, and employer sponsored events).

You can then start to plan for upcoming events in good time, highlighting all the important events you should attend.

Understand how international students are supported – Find out how the Careers Service supports international students (e.g. Are you allocated to a particular advisor? Do advisors have specific career specialisms?).

If you can choose any advisor, then I would suggest looking up their biographies (assuming they are available on the intranet) to identify those with relevant experience in the sectors that interest you. For instance, if you are considering a career in media and technology, you can ask for an appointment with the advisor with relevant experience.

An advisor with direct experience in the sectors you are interested in will be better able to:

(a) Provide specific and up-to-date advice and;

(b) Share employer contacts that may help further your career.

Schedule an appointment with an advisor – After you have identified an advisor with the relevant industry experience, schedule an initial appointment to discuss your career plans. Use this appointment as an opportunity to find out as much as possible about the industry you're interested in and where you can find additional information. If possible, use it to have an initial discussion about your CV and how you can start "beefing it up."

I would advise you not to consider this appointment as a one-off, but rather the start of a relationship with someone who can really help you on your career journey over the next couple of years.

When I look back to my student days at Cardiff University, I realise that I was fortunate to have had a wonderful careers advisor named Joanne. When I attended my first appointment, I barely had a CV or any understanding about a career in law or financial services. However, through a series of regular appointments throughout my time at university, she helped me develop a sound career plan, polish up my CV and provided useful industry contacts. She also helped review my application forms and prepare for interviews. From my experience, I have found that having a supportive Careers Advisor made a significant difference on my career prospects. I would advise students to establish good relationships with their careers advisors as it is likely to benefit you in your career journey.

3. Meet regularly with your personal tutor

Personal tutors are members of the academic staff that are normally assigned to assist you throughout your time at university. Typically, your personal tutor may schedule at least one appointment with you each term to find out how you are getting on at university. However, academics can be quite busy and have many other obligations (including looking after other students).

In reality, it is up to you to take the initiative and make the "personal tutor" relationship work for your benefit. That means you need to be proactive and schedule appointments as required. My advice about the personal tutor relationship is that you approach it in a similar way as your careers advisor – consider it a long-term relationship that will continue even after you finish university.

Your personal tutor is likely to become one of the references you will need when applying for jobs early in your career. Most graduate applications will require at least one academic reference. Moreover, most students are unlikely to have any work experience, so there is a lot of reliance on your personal tutor as a reference. You will also need references from your personal tutor for many other applications later in your career including: postgraduate applications, scholarships, applications to join professional bodies and many more.

You should build a good relationship with them so they get to know you well and, ideally, have a favourable view about your capabilities. This is important because the better your relationship, the more likely that they will support you as you build your career.

If you don't have a good relationship with your personal tutor, you are likely to get the standard (bland) template recommendation that says something about your grades at university and nothing more. These standard references will not help your application to stand out from the competition. However, if you cultivate a good relationship with your tutor, you are more likely to get a glowing and supportive reference.

Your personal tutor may also have very strong links with employers. If they have a favourable impression of you, they may help you connect with opportunities or projects that are not widely known.

Besides your assigned personal tutor, I would recommend that you find at least two more tutors. These additional tutors could be lecturers you get to know very well (e.g. because you took their modules or they supervised you on a particular project).

In simple terms, think of a tutor who you think knows you well and has a good understanding about your career goals and capabilities. You may also consider a tutor who has expertise and strong links in a speciality you are interested in. The key to this is that you need to be proactive and take the initiative. If you think a certain lecturer/professor would make a great tutor, set up an initial appointment and take it on from there.

4. Find a part-time job

I would advise that you take up a part-time job. Not only will this benefit you financially, it will also help you start to fill out your CV with relevant experience.

Part-time employment will help you feel more integrated with British culture as you interact with customers and colleagues. It will prepare you better for your future career. Your confidence will grow as you engage with people from all walks of life in the workplace.

You will gain more professional references that you can use later on when you apply for vacation schemes, internships or graduate roles.

5. Network widely

Make the most of your first year to build your personal network of friends and colleagues. You don't have to be restricted to people in the same academic department. Be open-minded and socialise beyond the default circle of people (flat mates, desk buddies, tutorial group).

As you do this, you are likely to make many life-long friendships with people who have similar goals, who challenge you or spur you on your career journey. As your network expands you can exchange and share intelligence, collaborate and form teams for business competitions.

Through these networks, you may even establish friendships that later become business partnerships. After all, there are plenty of examples of successful ventures that started as university friendships.

6. Explore entrepreneurship opportunities

There is significant interest today, particularly within the millennial generation, to pursue careers as entrepreneurs. There are several reasons entrepreneurship may be a popular career option. For some, it is a lifestyle choice, and the appeal of starting and owning your own business comes from the autonomy of working for yourself or "being your own boss."

For others, it may be about exploiting opportunities or gaps they see in the market for new or enhanced products and services. Arguably, advancements in technology today have increased the opportunities available for tech-savvy individuals to run successful ventures with nothing else but a website or a mobile app.

Entrepreneurship is constantly evolving and developing different labels or categories, including:

(a) Digital entrepreneurship – where services and products are created and delivered using digital channels online or mobile;

(b) Social entrepreneurship – start-up ventures that are focused on solving social, cultural or environmental problems;

(c) Intrapreneurship – the application of enterprise skills and skills within an existing company or organisation.

Despite the entrepreneurial aspirations of many students, a report by the *Centre for Entrepreneurs* shows that the start-up rates amongst graduates is low, compared to the potential and interest. This suggests that a lot of student entrepreneurial potential is underdeveloped or lost by graduation – even when university should be an ideal time to develop the entrepreneurial skills and attributes.

One reason for the failure to successfully develop entrepreneurial potential may be due to lack of support from universities. However, another reason may be that students do not realise that they need to be proactive at university in seeking opportunities that will help translate their entrepreneurial aspirations into reality.

Your first year of university is a great time to start exploring your entrepreneurship potential through light-touch activities as outlined below:

- Presentations or talks by entrepreneurs – Attend talks and presentations given by entrepreneurs. These sessions are typically organised by the careers service or individual faculties and may involve evening or day-time presentations.

These sessions can be very inspiring, particularly when you hear first-hand accounts about the experiences of notable entrepreneurs with well-established businesses.

I recall attending an engaging presentation by Dragon's Den star Nick Jenkins, where he shared his experience about founding *Moonpig.com*. These presentations can also be a great opportunity to network with other budding entrepreneurs, ask questions and gain a better understanding about what it takes to become an entrepreneur.

I would recommend signing up to email/mobile alerts from the careers service about upcoming presentations. Also, regularly check faculty and the careers service notice boards for scheduled presentations.

- Entrepreneurship awareness workshops – Attend entrepreneurship workshops organised by the university. These workshops may be organised by the careers service, student societies or through academic faculties such as the business school. Such workshops can help you acquire knowledge and understanding of enterprising activities. Ideally, there will be a range of workshops available including introductory sessions tailored to those with limited knowledge about entrepreneurship.

- Entrepreneurship clubs and societies – Join an entrepreneurship club where you can meet other like-minded students and get involved in a range of activities where you can engage with enterprise activity. Entrepreneurship clubs will give you the benefit of any events that are exclusive to members. Through your involvement with the club, you will also quickly gather intelligence and insights about the university's entrepreneurial activities (information that may not be easily accessible to non-members).

- <u>Business competitions</u> – There are numerous business competitions open to university students every year, including: business plan competitions and case study competitions.

I would recommend that you focus on building up your knowledge about entrepreneurship in your first year, with the aim of applying that knowledge and testing your ideas through business competitions in your penultimate year. For this reason, I will cover business competitions in more detail in the next section ("Penultimate Year").

You could start your preparation to participate in business competitions by doing research and gathering ideas about what you could do. For instance, find out if your university hosts any competitions. Enquire about these events with the Careers Service, the Entrepreneurship society or the Business School.

It is worth attending these events, which are often open to non-participating students, to get an idea of what it is like to pitch your ideas and compete against other students. During the presentations at these competitions, you are likely to pick up useful tips you can apply later when you participate.

7. Vacation schemes

As you formalise a plan for the careers and industries you are interested in, you should start to build a picture about the recruitment pipeline. Certain sectors or vocations like law will have a career timeline that opens up in the first year. For instance, there may be Christmas or Easter work experience opportunities or vacation schemes aimed at First Year students.

The *High Fliers Research* report for 2018 notes that more employers are developing work experience programmes for first year students. These may include open days, taster experiences and introductory courses.

If you're still caught up in the daze of an extended Freshers' week, you will miss the early application deadlines. Competition for vacation schemes is fierce during the penultimate year.

Getting a work experience scheme in your first year will give you the edge when applying for internships and placements later on. We will go into more detail about how to make these applications in later sections of the book.

 Useful information and resources

- **Prospects UK** provides guidance for students and graduates in relation to graduate careers. Their website provides a useful starting point when searching for work experience and internships:
  https://www.prospects.ac.uk/jobs-and-work-experience/work-experience-and-internships

- **Target Jobs** is another useful source of information when searching for work experience:
  https://targetjobs.co.uk/internships

- **Graduate Talent Pool** is a government-backed initiative designed to help students and graduates to gain work experience. You can find paid internships on their website:
  https://graduatetalentpoolsearch.direct.gov.uk

8. Do not neglect your academics

It is important to ensure you stay on top of your academics. For some courses, your first-year results will count towards your final degree result.

Applications for vacation schemes and internships often rely on academic results from your first and second year. So even though your first-year results do not count towards the final award, they will be critical for vacation scheme applications.

Additionally, start to consider what elective subjects you will choose for the remainder of your course. Ideally, consider courses or modules that align to your career objectives. For instance, if you are interested in commercial law, then you could select electives that show you have a strong interest, e.g. corporate law.

If you are interested in pursuing certain professional vocations, ensure that the modules you choose include any "mandatory modules." For instance, if you are interested qualifying as an accountant and are required to complete post-graduate qualifications, find out if there are undergraduate modules you can complete that would grant you future exemptions.

Furthermore, if you are interested in pursuing a professional vocation in your home country or another country, ensure that any mandatory modules are included in your undergraduate degree. Aligning your future vocational plans to your undergraduate study will help prevent a prolonged and expensive route to achieving the desired professional qualifications.

Entrepreneurship success story: Launching a ride-sharing company in India

 Raghav Tejpal (India)

Raghav is the founder and CEO of Greenerace Technologies, the company behind Bono Ride (BONO). BONO is a peer-to-peer ride-sharing (Carpooling) platform that enables people to travel together. The idea for a carpooling business came to Raghav whilst he was still at Cranfield University, where he completed his studies in Business and Administration.

He can still recall the day he was having a drink with his wife Truchi at the university pub, when decided to call the venture "BONO". At that point in time, the idea was nothing more than a few sheets of paper outlining the business plan and projections. However, within two years, BONO had developed into a start-up business with 20,000 registered customers completing on average over 450 rides each day. Raghav shares his experience and provides useful advice for students with entrepreneurial ambitions.

1. **What was your motivation for entrepreneurship instead of being employed?**

   When I commenced my university study, I honestly wasn't certain about what I would do after I graduated. Initially, my career plan was consisted of aspirations for senior management roles within an established company and then, after a few years I could start a business (once I had substantial savings). It was clear to me that my university experience would not just be about learning the business skills I needed but it was also about embarking on a journey of continuous self-discovery and improvement.

During that journey, I learnt a lot about myself and how I work with others. I realised that I enjoyed trying to find solutions to seemingly intractable problems, and I excelled at it. I also discovered that if I was to reach the full potential of my talents, it was absolutely essential to have autonomy. In my view, it is better to focus on your strengths when choosing your career because that will increase your chances of success and provide satisfaction.

It became obvious to me that even if I obtained employment with an established organisation, I will always have a strong desire to become an entrepreneur. My university experience provided many useful opportunities to test and develop the attributes and skills that would be essential for an entrepreneurship career.

Whilst at university, I formed a team with two of my classmates and we entered the *Hult Sustainability Challenge* - one of the world's largest student competitions. Our team was successful in this competition and went all the way to the finals. We also participated in our university's *Start-up Weekend*, where our team excelled and emerged as the first runner's up. I really enjoyed these experiences and learnt a lot about developing solutions to problems and how to build various components of a business from scratch. As a result, I became drawn more to the idea of starting a business sooner.

There were a few business ideas that I had been harbouring, but I lacked the courage to take the first step and start transforming those ideas into viable ventures.

I continued to seek employment, even when I knew deep down that I was not being true to myself and actually wanted a completely different future.

In preparation for my job applications, I had a mock interview with someone who had had substantial leadership experience. After an hour-long interview he told me that he would not have considered me for the position. This wasn't because he doubted my skill, but because he felt that it would only be a matter of time before I left the job, even if I was successful. This was exactly what I needed to hear.

I wanted to create elegant solutions, I wanted to be challenged and I wanted to do things which are akin to my own personality and talents. I discussed my predicament with my wife and once she agreed to support me on my decision, I never again thought of getting employed. I became determined and committed to becoming an entrepreneur and focussed on working on it with all my heart.

2. **What key factors would you advise students who are interested in becoming entrepreneurs to consider when they are choosing a UK university?**

I would advise prospective students to do thorough research to understand whether the universities that they are considering will be beneficial for their entrepreneurial aspirations.

Firstly, I would recommend that students should try to understand whether the university has a well-developed start-up ecosystem. An integral part of this ecosystem is the availability of entrepreneurship mentors. I was fortunate in this regard because the Course Leader was also our lecturer on entrepreneurship and she was passionate about start-ups. The guidance that she provided during the early stages helped me get the fundamentals right. It also gave me the confidence to start my venture much earlier than I had initially planned.

Students should research the types of entrepreneurship events that the university hosts or supports. This can be a good indicator of how committed the institution is to entrepreneurship and how much support you could expect in developing your start-up ideas. My first real step towards entrepreneurship was the university's *Start-up Weekend*, which later propelled me to other such events.

Students should also enquire about recent graduates and alumni who have gone on to become entrepreneurs. If possible, students can then reach out to alumni to understand the kind of support they received at university.

Students should also try to find out whether about the networks of business angels and venture capitalists that are affiliated with the university. These networks can be very beneficial, enabling aspiring entrepreneurs to find funding and expertise. Students should also ensure that the university's entrepreneurial focus is in line with your aspirations.

3. **If you had the chance to do it all again, what would you do differently?**

With the benefit of hindsight, we can all see things that we could have done differently. That being said, I recognise that my university experience was also an evolutionary process that was necessary to developing the conviction that I have towards my business today. However, I do think I could have got more out of university if I had done two things differently.

a) *Having a clear goal right from the start:* By the second quarter of my course, I was actively participating in entrepreneurial competitions and events. However, my approach towards my education changed significantly when I actually started working on a business idea. I spent a few months researching and building on the idea of producing and selling Cider drinks in India. I took it to a point where I started receiving investor interest and I was almost ready to start that venture.

During this period, I found myself analysing and applying the management principles, I was learning in class, directly to my work. I also got more clarity on the components from my course that I would need to invest more time on. I think if I had made the decision to become an entrepreneur sooner, I could have got a lot more from my university experience.

b) *Expect your business ideas to be challenged:* The second thing that I would do differently is that I would not let emotions cloud my judgment. Later during my course, I decided not to go ahead with the cider business and turned my attention to the ride-sharing business that I run now. I went through the process of developing the business plan and was as sure of its success then, as I am of it now.

Unfortunately I took it too personally when a faculty member and mentor did not understand my passion for the business. I decided not to consult them again, even when I knew it would help my business progress faster.

Later in my entrepreneurial journey I would realise that people's opinions are only based on the information they have at a certain point in time and those opinions often change when circumstances do. One of the angel investors, who did not support my idea initially, eventually became an investor in my company. This would not have happened if I had not learned from my previous experience.

4. **What are the highlights and challenges that you can share about starting your own business?**

The value of persistence: By the time my course was ending, I had the first draft of my ride-sharing business plan ready. In the months that followed, I tried to convince people to invest in this venture. However, this was much harder than I thought it would be. None of my friends and family seemed too keen to invest in the idea. My university network, which seemed to back my initial idea (the Cider business), was unimpressed and critical of about my idea for a carpooling business. Many people I spoke to were dismissive, stating that "Carpooling can never work." Since the environmental aspect of "sharing" was one of the key elements of our proposition, some potential investors declared that "no one in India cares for the Environment".

Initially I found this very discouraging, but then I realised it was all part of the challenges that came with entrepreneurship. Within a few months, I was able to raise enough capital to ensure that the development would be taken care of. This experience helped me to realise that although things can get tough, even impossible at times, but persistence will always pay off.

Building a team: I was able to convince an old colleague of mine, Dinesh, to help me build a technology team. Dinesh had more than a decade of experience in technology and was one of the most efficient people I had worked with in the past. Eventually, Dinesh left his Job at Xerox and joined BONO full-time. My classmate Preetham, was initially involved in helping me to review my business plan and projections. However, he became drawn more into the idea and later decided to become a part of this venture.

I returned to India from the UK, registered a company, and started recruiting for more talent. However, I discovered that it was challenging for start-ups to attract good talent because many job seekers were seeking for stability and wished to be associated with established brand-names. As a result, some start-ups are willing to pay higher salaries to employees.

However, this can be a big mistake as remuneration alone is not a lasting incentive. It is always better to build a team of people who are intrinsically motivated and connect with the idea. I had to be very patient before I could have the right people However; it was not long before we had a functional team of talented and motivated people.

Managing expenditure: The value of being frugal cannot be overstated in the context of start-ups. We made a few mistakes in the beginning and overspent. Although it didn't seem like overspending at that time, I now understand that much of this could have been avoided. It is vital for start-ups to have a grip on their finances and only spend on what is absolutely necessary.

Prioritise your goals: Many fledgling businesses make the mistake of trying to achieve too many goals at once because they want to grow quickly. The idea of acquiring a sizable customer base seems very tempting and many start-ups go for it even before they have thoroughly understood customer behaviours.

It is better to work with a smaller number of customers and perfect your solution before going to a wider audience. There have been numerous highs and lows in developing the business to where it is today. Making the right judgment calls can be tough but my guiding principle has been to ensure that the best interests of the business are given the higher priority.

The importance of resilience: As an entrepreneur, I have had to develop a lot of resilience to overcome all the challenges thrown at me. Developing a business with limited resources has meant making hard decisions such as limiting the level of salaries that directors can take to plough finances back into the business. Dealing with a personal tragedy at a time when my business was facing a potential cash-crunch was one of the most difficult situations that I have faced. My father passed away suddenly and during that time, I remember feeling very sad and responsible for the difficult predicament that my family was facing.

Although the outlook seemed bleak at the time, I resolved never to give up. I told myself that my father would be proud of a son who doesn't give up. It may sound like an emotional decision, but it isn't. In my view if there is no possible course of action that will take me to the desired outcome, then I must stop. Otherwise there is no reason to quit. Quitting something, just to avoid the discomfort of pain, even when you know that success can be achieved, is an emotional decision.

I managed to get out of that difficult situation, and the business has made tremendous progress since then. The number of rides has almost doubled and the future prospects are looking much brighter. I can envisage a future where millions of people will happily carpool on BONO.

5. **What pearls of wisdom do you have for budding entrepreneurs whilst they are at university? In particular, how would you advise them about maximising their university experience so that they can launch entrepreneurship ventures?**

- *Network widely at university:* You have such a wonderful opportunity to meet many talented people from diverse walks of life. Talk to people and share your ideas. Who knows, maybe some of your friends and colleagues at university may become long-term business partners. That's what happened to me.

- *Participate in business competitions:* Business competitions are a tremendous opportunity for you to test your ideas and build the skills that will be vital to become a successful entrepreneur. Take full advantage and take part in any national or international competitions. Even if you don't emerge as a winner, you will develop the skills you need as an entrepreneur, your confidence will grow and its great fun too.

You can find more information about Raghav and his company at: *www.bonoride.com.*

CHAPTER 5

Penultimate year

"Juggling is the word. I'm a bad juggler, and there are often balls dropped. There is no balance. The idea of work/life balance is a myth. There's teetering from one end and running to the other and hoping not to fall off."
– Sonya Walger

By the time you start your penultimate year, your CV should start to look beefier already, assuming you have been actively updating it with all the activities from your first year (see preceding chapter). You should also have a better idea about what career sectors you are interested in. By this time, your confidence about living in the UK will have increased and you will be more comfortable with British culture.

In your penultimate year, expect the intensity to ramp up in relation to preparing for a graduate career. It will feel busier because many vacation schemes and internships are aimed at penultimate students. If you are on a degree course with a sandwich placement (industrial placement), your penultimate year is when you should start applying for placements.

Furthermore, there are a number of graduate schemes that are targeted towards penultimate students that open in the summer before your final year. Law firms, for instance, typically recruit future trainees two years before they start their training contracts. There are other graduate schemes that follow similar timelines.

Therefore, the period after you start the penultimate year right through the summer can feel very "application-heavy." You could find yourself juggling lots of different applications, attending recruitment events and interviews, whilst also staying on top of your academic commitments.

Figure 2: Juggling numerous responsibilities

If you get it right, however, all this effort will pay off handsomely – and you may find yourself in the enviable position of having a lucrative graduate scheme lined up before you graduate. If you are fortunate enough to have secured a graduate offer by the end of your penultimate year, it will take a huge weight off your shoulders as you go into the final year.

Let us look at some of the actions you should take to maximise your penultimate year.

Actions to advance your career development

i. Get involved in co-curricular activities

Join a university society or club, if you haven't already done so, as this will help your career prospects (see preceding chapter). If you are already a member of a university society, consider whether your involvement so far has been active, with a demonstrable level of responsibility.

If you haven't been active, then your penultimate year should be the year you step up your involvement, e.g. by taking on a leadership role. If all you've been doing so far is turn up for meetings and events, then this is the year you should consider taking on some responsibility.

Active involvement in co-curricular activity will help you develop many of the competencies you will need in your future career. It will enhance your CV and prospective applications and give you meaningful examples to use when you are interviewed. Furthermore, it will help you enjoy your student experience as you contribute to university life.

ii. Utilise the Careers Service

Schedule an appointment with the Careers Service early in the term. Find out what events/activities are planned for the year so you can schedule relevant events in your calendar.

Organise an appointment with your Careers Advisor so you can discuss your objectives for the year and devise a plan to achieve them. Have your CV reviewed and follow up any recommended amendments.

You should let your advisor know which industries you are interested in and the vacation schemes you want to target. If you

159

already know the deadlines for some applications, this would be a good opportunity to schedule future appointments to have your draft applications reviewed. Keep your advisor updated with your progress so that if necessary, you can schedule further appointments to help you as your application progresses (e.g. with interview preparation).

iii. Meet-up with your personal tutors

Make appointments with your personal tutors early in the term so they are aware of your plans and can advise you on your strategy. Your first appointment in the term is a great opportunity to review your progress academically and in relation to your career plans.

You will also need their support as potential references for any applications you make during the term. Academic tutors can be very busy and will appreciate the early heads-up on any requests for references.

iv. Participate in entrepreneurship activities

If you are considering entrepreneurship as a career option, please refer to the previous section on *"Explore entrepreneurship opportunities."* The activities outlined in this section will be relevant for your penultimate year as well.

Business competitions – Register to participate in internal or external business competitions. Every year, there are numerous UK and international competitions open to university students, including venture competitions, business plan competitions, case competitions and science competitions.

These competitions are usually organised or sponsored by leading companies and offer students the opportunity to enrich their university experience by solving real-world problems. These competitions offer students the opportunity to test their business ideas, build their creative and innovative skills and collaborate in multi-disciplinary teams.

There is a lot of prestige in winning these competitions (with prize money ranging from £1k to £10k+) or emerging as a finalist. If you don't make it to the finals of a competition, you will still benefit from participation, as the experience will sharpen your entrepreneurial skills and attributes and enhance your CV. Even if you decide not to become an entrepreneur, the experience can enhance your CV and prove to be advantageous when you apply for graduate positions with companies.

 Useful information and resources

Here are some useful online resources for finding competitions:

- **Student competitions.com** is a website which aggregates international competitions from around the world for students. You can access this website via the following link: *https://studentcompetitions.com/*

- **The Case centre.org** provides a list of case competitions that students can enter. You can search the student pages on the following website to find available competitions: *https://www.thecasecentre.org/main/*

You should also keep checking the careers service and business school notice boards for competitions or any internal competitions or small/local competitions that may not be widely advertised.

v. Attend careers fairs and campus recruitment events

Ensure that you noted all the key recruitment events in your calendar. In advance of your attendance, do your research on potential employers represented at these events. This will prepare you to have meaningful conversations as you are networking.

First impressions count, and it is possible that the people you meet at these events could be the same people who end up interviewing you. If you make a favourable impression, it may make the difference in whether your application is successful or not.

Useful information and resources for careers fairs

- The Institute of Student Employers (ISE), formerly the Association of Graduate Recruiters (AGR), provides details about careers fairs around the country: *https://ise.org.uk/*

vi. Part-time work

Depending on your financial situation and how much work experience you have gained, you may consider de-prioritising part-time employment. Your penultimate year will be busy, so you want to ensure that you are not overstretched and stressed by taking on a part-time job.

However, if you don't have any work experience on your CV, then a part-time job may be beneficial. It may also be a necessity, if you need the job to pay for your living expenses.

vii. Apply for vacation schemes and internships

As mentioned earlier, your penultimate year will be a busy one as you start applying for vacation schemes. You should have a list of the vacation schemes you are interested in and know their recruitment timeline so that you do not miss any deadlines.

It would be advantageous for you to apply for the Christmas vacation schemes, as they are not as popular as the Easter and summer schemes. Additionally, give yourself the head-start on your peers by applying for the schemes with early deadlines.

Postgraduate study

Postgraduate study is very popular with international students. According to the Higher Education Statistical Agency (HESA), the proportion of international students undertaking postgraduate study in the UK was 42%.

As many international students go straight into postgraduate study after they have completed their undergraduate degree, it is appropriate to briefly cover this here. I should make it clear that postgraduate study is an immense topic in itself. So the considerations noted below are by no means exhaustive.

If you are determined to undertake postgraduate study immediately after your bachelor's degree, you should research your options in good time. Although it seems early to be researching postgraduate options, remember that postgraduate admission starts a year in advance of the course start. This means early deadlines for applications will be at the beginning of your final year.

Popular postgraduate courses will have shorter timeframes for their admissions process. It is quite common for programme tutors to close applications before the deadline (as soon as they have enough applications). To give yourself enough time to research your options and have your application ready, start the groundwork during your penultimate year.

If you are not planning to start a postgraduate immediately after your bachelor's degree, then you have more time and do not need to start researching in your penultimate year.

There are a variety of reasons students consider postgraduate study. The main reasons include:

- To pursue careers in academia: Postgraduate research degrees or doctoral level qualifications are often pre-requisites for careers in higher education, e.g. lecturing or academic research.

- Intellectual curiosity: Some students pursue further studies because of the enjoyment they derive from studying particular subjects. During undergraduate study, students may develop a deep interest in certain topics and seek to delve into more detail through postgraduate study.

- Vocational requirement: Certain careers stipulate postgraduate qualifications as a part of their professional requirements, e.g. to qualify as a barrister or solicitor.

- Enhance your career prospects: A postgraduate qualification could enhance your CV and career prospects by giving you an advantage over the competition.

Whatever your motivation, you should give careful consideration to whether postgraduate study will be advantageous for your career. The timing of your postgraduate study should also be a key consideration. For instance, would it be more beneficial to gain work experience after your undergraduate degree before pursuing another degree?

You may find yourself at a disadvantage if you specialise in a particular subject, achieve numerous qualifications and then later on discover that you dislike a career in that sector. Remember that postgraduate qualifications can be taken at a later stage in your career.

There are tremendous benefits to gaining some industry knowledge and work experience before you commence a postgraduate qualification. These include the following:

- You are more likely to have a better idea about your long-term career goals.

- You will gain more value from the course by drawing on your industry knowledge and professional experience.

- You are more likely to be in a better financial position to fund postgraduate study (e.g. employer sponsorship, self-funding from savings).

- Recruiters also value postgraduate qualifications more when it is backed by sufficient work experience. It shows maturity and commitment to pursue a particular career path.

 Key points to remember when considering whether to pursue postgraduate study

- Ensure that you are clear about your reasons for pursuing postgraduate study.

- Further study may be beneficial if: (a) you need the qualification to get into a certain vocation; (b) you have a strong interest in the subject; (c) you are considering a career in academia; (d) you want to enhance your long-term career prospects.

- Do not rush into postgraduate study because: (a) you are not sure what you want after your undergraduate degree; or (b) you wish to delay starting your career.

- Remember, you can always pursue further studies later in your career.

- Consider the advantages of having industry experience before you pursue further studies. Further qualifications look more attractive on your CV when complimented with relevant work experience.

Managing your busy schedule

With your academic and career activities getting busier, it is likely that you will face some scheduling dilemmas. Common scheduling dilemmas include: (a) being offered interview dates that fall on the same dates that you have major assignments or assessments due; (b) getting offers for different interviews on the same date; (c) receiving offers for an internship or graduate role, whilst you are still interviewing for other roles.

Let us consider ways you can manage these challenges.

(a) Clashes between academic and career commitments – Students are likely to face situations where the demands from academic commitments are at odds with career activities. One reason you need to build a good rapport with your tutors and keep your academic tutors updated about the progress of your applications is so they can support you in these situations.

Tutors can be very understanding and help you manage difficult dilemmas. For instance, if you have an assignment due on a date that you have been offered an interview, you could seek an extension from the relevant programme leader (with the backing of your tutor). Good recruiters also realise that students have academic commitments and will usually offer alternative dates that are more suitable.

You may find you have to miss the occasional lecture or tutorial to attend recruitment events, open days, interviews, etc. In these situations, it is advisable to let the lecturer or tutor know. It would help to demonstrate how you will catch up with what you have missed in class (e.g. submit tutorial assignments at a later date). Your colleagues can also be invaluable during these times by helping you to keep up with anything you may have missed in lectures.

(b) <u>Different interviews on the same date</u> – If you are offered two interviews on the same date, you could first see if it is possible to have one in the morning and another in the afternoon. However, be mindful about whether it is logistically possible (e.g. this might not be viable if the interviews are in different cities). You could also explore whether alternative dates could be an option.

Check with the recruiter to see whether there is some flexibility on dates. You do not have to tell them that you have another interview elsewhere. Prioritise your preferred employer (i.e., try and reschedule the appointment being offered by the other company first).

(c) <u>Receiving an offer whilst interviewing for others</u> – Many students worry about the situation where they get an offer from one employer, whilst still interviewing or expecting offers for other opportunities. In the unlikely event you find yourself in this situation, remember that a firm and unconditional offer from one employer is far better than the mere possibility of an offer from another employer.

(d) It is not advisable to tell the employer making you the firm offer that you want to wait and see what another employer will offer. The employer making the offer may find this insulting and could easily withdraw the offer, leaving you with nothing.

 Deadlines to watch out for

Law: If you are interested in becoming a solicitor, you need to be aware of early deadlines. Law firms start recruiting two years in advance. Deadlines for training contract applications tend to fall in the summer before you start your final year, typically by 31 July.

For additional information, visit the Solicitors Regulation Authority: *https://www.sra.org.uk/students/students.page*

Graduate success story: Ronald (Uganda)

 Ronald (Uganda)

Ronald came to the UK as an overseas student from Uganda. He studied E-commerce and Digital Business at Nottingham University. After graduating he worked in Uganda for two years before pursuing further studies in the UK. Since completing his studies, he has developed a successful career in data analytics. He shares his experience and provides useful advice for prospective and current students.

1. **Why did you decide to study in the UK?**

   I completed my A Levels in the UK, so it was a natural progression. I did my A levels in the UK, due to my school in Kenya having good links with UK schools.

2. **What factors influenced your choice of university?**

   I considered the reputation/ranking, provision of the course I wanted to do and a university outside of London.

3. **What influenced your decision to choose the course you took?**

   I had done work experience in the field I originally wanted to do (accounting), but felt I was better suited to a course with a business background and computer science mix due to my strength in maths.

4. **Did your university experience match your expectations?**

   Not quite, the course was more computer science heavy and focused on the programming and practical elements. I was looking for a more holistic course that covered theory,

169

programming and business elements. However, my course was limited to two modules of business each semester. I was also in a class with people who had more advanced programming skills, so lecturers used to pass over certain areas which they felt were basic but were not for people who did not have BTEC qualifications.

5. **How useful was the university careers service in helping you secure a job?**

The university careers office was useful, with CV clinics and hosting events with employers. I was less active in my use of these, and I missed out on internships in my second year. It may have helped if a career guide plan had been put in place to let students know the importance of internships at the end of their second year, but I was not proactive enough until my final year when it was maybe too late.

6. **Describe your job hunting experience in the UK.**

I found it very difficult. I graduated in the period just after the post work visa was abolished, so getting a place in a company in the tight immigration climate was hard.

I applied for some graduate schemes and attended several employer events on campus. If I could go back, I would have been more proactive between January and March in my penultimate year as I feel that an internship that summer would have done me a world of good for experience.

At around Easter time in my final year, I made the decision to move home once my graduation was complete after failing with over 12 applications. This was also due to not having spent much time in Uganda during my childhood and schooling, having lived in the UK from the age of 4 to 11, then in boarding school (Kenya) all the way up to university. With my time there, I would aim to gain experience and then return to the UK to complete a master's and then try again to crack the UK job market.

7. What advice do you have for prospective students to help them make the most out of the university experience?

I suggest visiting the careers office and getting your CV and cover letter checked as soon as possible. Then also register your interest in potential employers' companies in your penultimate year to show that you are proactive and desire to work with those companies. However, I also advise students to be patient when they start applying for jobs and receiving rejections. Get over the rejections and move on! Don't let rejections bring you down. Remember that many people will submit 10+ applications, with the majority getting rejected.

CHAPTER 6

The recruitment process

With applications for vacation schemes and graduate schemes expected to start during your penultimate year, it is appropriate to cover all the essentials of the recruitment process in this section.

The selection process for vacation schemes and graduate schemes is quite similar. Today, many recruiters use their vacation schemes as the recruitment pool for their future graduates.

Therefore, competition for vacation schemes is probably more intense and selective, compared to the graduate schemes. The guidance in this section will apply to recruitment on vacation placements/internships and graduate schemes.

Essentially, there are three key stages in the recruitment process: (a) application form (which may include CV and cover letter); (b) interviews; and (c) assessment centres. Many leading employers tend to follow this format, but there can be slight variations between different employers.

For instance, the number and types of interviews can vary with some having interviews before or after the assessment centre.

In reality, the selection process works like a funnel as a large volume of applications is gradually whittled down to the lucky few to whom offers will be made (figure 3). One leading employer is reported to have received 37,000 applications for 1,600 positions in 2017. This illustrates the intensity of competition in the graduate market.

Figure 3: The Recruitment Funnel

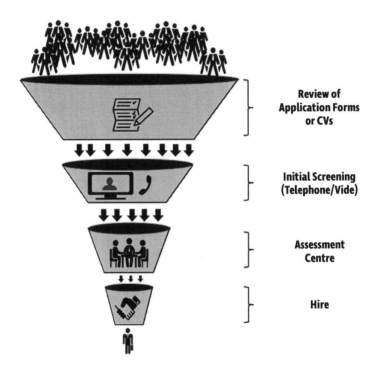

Let us look at the recruitment process in more detail.

Application forms and CVs

Selection for vacation or graduate schemes today will typically involve the completion of an online application form. Some applications may ask you to also attach your CV. The requirement to provide a CV has been done away with for most vacation or graduate schemes. However, that is not to say that there is no benefit to having an up-to-date CV.

In fact, your CV is a good starting point for drafting your application form and a lot of the information you provide in the form will be readily available. The CV is also useful for networking, giving potential recruiters a snapshot of your skills and achievements to date.

As the first stage in the selection process, the application form is where most rejections will occur as recruiters seek to identify the most suitable candidates to advance to the next stage. Modern online application forms can be read electronically, enabling early electronic screening on a points system. If the application form does not meet the criteria to pass this electronic screening, it will be automatically rejected even before a recruiter can review it.

1. Distinguish yourself from the competition

Now you know most candidates are rejected from the selection process based on their applications, you need to devise a strategy to ensure you have every chance of success at this stage. The first and most important question you need to ask yourself is: What makes my CV or application stand out from everyone else? In other words, think about how you can demonstrate your unique attributes so they stand out clearly in your application or CV.

Advertisers often refer to the "unique selling points" (USP) of a product or service as those qualities that make a particular product or service distinct (and preferably more desirable than others). The concept of a USP is useful to consider when applying for careers. Think about yourself in those terms and consider why an employer would want to consider your application over others – i.e., what are your USPs?

As you draft your CV, even before you make your application, spend some time outlining your unique qualities, key strengths and achievements. These attributes may include achievement of awards or special recognition at university, internship opportunities that stand out, fluency in certain foreign languages, etc. When you have outlined the unique qualities that make you stand out, ensure that they feature prominently in your CV or application form.

2. Essential features of an effective CV

An effective CV should have the following sections and information included:

(a) Personal Details - This is the first section of your CV and should include your name, address (including postcode), telephone number(s) and email address. Remember to use a professional looking email address, e.g. "*joebloggs@yahoo.com*" and not an address that is very informal and unlikely to be taken seriously, e.g. "*smartdude@gmail.com*."

(b) Personal Statement – This should be a short paragraph that encapsulates your unique skills and attributes. It is in this section that the reader will see that you stand out and will be prompted to read on. Three or four short sentences should be sufficient for this section.

(c) Education – Outline your schools and university education to date. Include the dates you attended. Include qualifications you have and may be working towards, including A-Levels. List your grades and any special academic awards/prizes next to your qualifications. You don't have to list all your GCSEs and should summarise them instead.

(d) Work Experience – Describe your work experience to date including the name of the employer, your job title and an outline of your role/responsibilities. Include dates and order this section starting with the most recent role you had. You could also include any volunteering opportunities or involvement in university societies. You should devote more space on the most recent roles instead of historic roles that may have little or no bearing on your future career.

(e) Skills – Outline the skills you have that may be useful in a job context, e.g. IT or software skills. You could also list any foreign language skills or useful qualifications that could be transferable to most employers (e.g. First Aid certification).

(f) Personal Interests – You can list extracurricular activities and hobbies. Recruiters want to hire well-rounded people who will fit in their organisation. Your personal interests can give them a view of the kind of person you are. This may be a good section to list the co-curricular activities that you may be involved in at university or achievements from school (e.g. Duke of Edinburgh Award). Think carefully about what hobbies you disclose here as certain hobbies may create an unfavourable impression.

(g) References – You are not required to list them on your CV. Instead, you can indicate that they are available on request.

Key points to remember about CVs

- **Personal statement:** Your personal statement is your opportunity to highlight your unique selling points and personalise your CV. It should make the reader eager to read the rest of your CV. You should briefly summarise key achievements and what you hope to achieve in the future. Remember, recruiters will focus their attention on the top half of the first page of your CV and their attention falls as they read down the page. By positioning your personal statement in the top half of the page, you ensure that they get to see your unique attributes to keep them interested in the rest of your CV.

- **Personal Details:** Ensure that your personal details are laid out clearly at the top of your CV. Also use a professional looking email address.

- **Presentation:** Use appropriate spacing between sections. It is advisable not to use font sizes smaller than 11 pt. Avoid bright or informal looking font types and be consistent with the style that you use.

- **Work Experience:** Include the name of the employer, role title and start/completion dates. List your work experience chronologically, starting with the most recent one at the top. Ensure that you mention what your actual responsibilities were.

- **Education:** Include key qualifications and achievements to date. Summarise your GCSEs. It is not necessary to include your primary school details.

- **Community engagement and volunteering:** Remember that undertaking any volunteering activity counts. If you have been involved or are still actively involved in these activities, indicate them on your CV.

- **References:** There is no need to list references on your CV, but make sure you have the contact details available if asked. Do not use relatives as referees.

- **Proofread:** It is important to check your CV for spelling and grammatical errors. Remember, first impressions count, so don't let your CV be rejected because of typos.

- **Personal interests:** Consider whether the interests that you have outlined are suitable for potential employers to see. Achievements from extracurricular activities are useful to outline in this section.

- **Be specific:** Avoid the temptation to fill out your CV with buzzwords but without being clear on what it is you did. Anyone can say they have "leadership" or "communication" skills. Recruiters are more interested in understanding what you actually achieved.

- **Length:** CVs should not be longer than two sides of A4 paper.

3. Completing application forms

It is important to give yourself enough time to prepare, review and complete the online application forms.

(a) Preparation – When you start your online application, ensure that you allow yourself sufficient time to complete it. The form will typically require details about your background and experience (i.e., information that may be covered in your CV that you may easily copy across).

However, there will also be essay-style questions that test your motivation and seek to draw out your skills and competencies. It is advisable to first complete these essay-type questions outside of the application form. For instance, you could copy the questions into MS Word, noting word count limit, and complete them there. This allows you to work outside of the application form, minimising the possibility of errors (clicking "submit" before it is complete, etc.). It may also be easier to proofread and check for grammatical errors.

Do your research on the company, the industry it operates in, and role you are applying for before you complete the form. This research should enable you to identify the qualities being sought after in applicants so you can match these to your skills and experience. Your answers should demonstrate that you have done your research and help your application to stand out. The answers you provide will need to show how you are suitably matched for the role and the company. Where possible, reflect the language and terminology used by the recruiter.

The specification for most roles will typically include *essential* criteria (i.e., the minimum standards expected in every candidate) and *desirable* criteria (i.e., the nice-to-have, optional extra qualities that employers seek but are not considered indispensable). For example, a job role may indicate fluency in English as an essential requirement and knowledge of Spanish as desirable.

Top tips for completing application forms

- Before completing you application, identify the essential and desirable criteria.

- Then, spend some time outlining the key aspects from your experience that match the essential and desirable criteria. This exercise will enable you to demonstrate your suitability for a particular role when you fill out your application.

- A good application will stand out because it is clear to the recruiter how the candidate matches up to the role.

(b) <u>Review</u> – Have your application reviewed by your careers adviser or even a close colleague or friend. They may help you identify errors and suggest ways to enhance your application. If there is a word count, ensure that you don't exceed it; otherwise, this will be an automatic rejection.

(c) <u>Complete</u> – After your offline draft application has been reviewed, copy all your answers into the online form. Review the entire application and save it as a draft. Then you should review the draft once again and submit when you are satisfied that there is nothing more you can do to enhance it any further.

Key points to remember about application forms

- **Answer the question:** Be careful that you actually answer the questions correctly. Avoid the temptation of recycling statements you have used in previous applications. Recruiters will know when you have simply copied a statement from a different application.

- **Relevance:** Ensure your answers show how your skills and attributes are a close match for the role and organisation that you are applying for. Thorough research before you complete the application is vital.

- **Check, check and check again:** Proofread your application and also ask someone else to review it before you submit.

- **Observe any specific requirements:** Ensure you follow any rules, including the word count or any formatting requests.

- **Keep it professional:** Ensure that the language you use is suitable, e.g. avoid abbreviations (unless clearly defined), slang, and text-speak.

Interviews

After applications have been reviewed, successful candidates will be invited to the next stage of selection; which usually means attending an interview. Getting through to the interview stage is no easy feat, as recruiters will have declined the vast majority of applications by this stage.

Being invited to attend the interview stage should fill you with confidence – recruiters have identified your potential and are interested in finding out more about you.

Interviews used to be conducted solely as face-to-face interviews. However, advances in technology and changes in recruitment practice have led to the emergence of a variety of different channels for conducting interviews. It is now commonplace to have multiple interviews for a particular role using a combination of different channels, i.e., telephone, face-to-face, or video.

For recruiters, the use of multiple interview channels has given them more tools to assess and compare applicants before final decisions are made. For students applying for roles, the reality is that the interview stage will actually involve multiple interviews using different channels. For some, students may consider this unnecessary and cumbersome because they have more hurdles to jump before they get to the desired end.

An alternative view is that this provides students more opportunities to consistently prove themselves as ideal candidates. Undoubtedly, this has made the selection process more competitive and challenging – hence the need for candidates to be as well prepared as possible.

In this section, we shall look at the different types of interviews and the key points candidates should know to maximise their opportunities for success.

Types of Interviews

The approach adopted by recruiters today is to use virtual interview channels before proceeding to a stage where face-to-face interaction takes place. Virtual channels in this context include telephone and video interviews. The advantage of adopting virtual channels is that it has helped reduce recruitment costs for both candidates and employers (e.g. by limiting travel expenses).

It has also been beneficial for candidates as some borderline applications may be allowed to go through to the next stage. When screening applications, recruiters will often have doubts about whether to progress certain applications. Rather than decline the application, they may use the virtual interview as a way of clarifying any areas of doubt before deciding to decline or progress.

1. Telephone Interviews

In most cases, a telephone interview will be scheduled as the next stage of assessment. In recent years, telephone interviews have grown in popularity as a way for recruiters to perform an initial screening of candidates, to check that the candidate meets the essential criteria for the role. In some cases, however, the telephone interview may test your motivation for the role and your interest in the organisation.

In most cases, the telephone interview will be a scheduled appointment and you will receive brief details about date and time for the call, who you will be speaking to and what the call is likely to cover. However, if you do not receive this information, then you would be advised to check whether you should expect a diarised interview.

 Top tips regarding telephone interviews

- **Check the information provided about the call:** Check the information provided about the call to understand whether the call will focus on specific areas and who you will be speaking to.

- **Review your application form:** It is highly likely that the entire call will be based on the details you have provided.

You would be surprised how some candidates forget what they wrote in their applications. Don't be that candidate who gets stumped because they can't remember what they put in their application.

- **Quiet location:** Ensure you have a quiet location for your call. If you live in shared accommodation, you should let your housemates know you are expecting a telephone interview so they can limit potential disturbance.

- **Have your application and notes nearby:** You should have your application form or CV on hand during the interview for easy reference.

- **Stay calm and smile:** Maintain a calm composure and remember to control your breathing. Telephone interviews can be quite unnerving for some people, bearing in mind how much is at stake. Do not panic if the call feels slightly awkward, especially at the beginning. Take your cues from the interviewer. Allow them to introduce themselves and explain how the call will proceed. Remember to smile; it will help you sound positive and enthusiastic.

- **Phone battery:** Remember to have your phone fully charged. The last thing you need is your battery going flat midway through the call.

2. Video interviews

The use of video interviews is on the rise in graduate applications. In some cases, the video interview is a short interview to probe or clarify certain aspects of the application (i.e., as an alternative to an audio-only call).

In other cases, the video interview may be more in-depth and could even be the final interview. However, this is likely to be in situations where the video interview is the only viable option (e.g. because the interviewer or the applicant is travelling abroad at the time). There are two types of video interviews.

(a) Pre-recorded videos - Firstly, there's the option of making pre-recorded videos in response to specific questions. This option is not a fully interactive two-way communication. They tend to involve timed recordings and may require that you register on an online portal or download certain software to enable the call.

(b) Live video - You could have a fully interactive video call where you interact in real-time (e.g. using Skype, FaceTime). This option tends to be used at a later stage in the selection process, where it is more convenient for the employer and the candidate.

 Top tips regarding video interviews

- **Computer requirements:** Check if there are any computer or software requirements relevant for the call. For pre-recorded videos, you may need to register on a portal or download software to enable the video call. If possible, test that the software actually works before you schedule the final videos.

- **Set the scene:** Be mindful about the setting for the recording. You may not want certain posters or parts of your student room to be on full display to potential employers.

- **Dress for the part:** Although it is a video, it is still a formal interview. Dress smartly like you would for a formal face-to-face interview.

- **Practice being on camera:** If you are not comfortable featuring in a video, you should spend time practising in front of your camera. This will help you build confidence in front of the camera.

- **Positive body language:** Body language accounts for 55% of your communication, so you need to ensure that it is positive. Remember to smile, sit up straight and keep hand movements to a minimum.

- **Written notes:** Exercise caution if you intend to rely on written notes. They could easily become distracting if you have to refer to them, which can be off-putting for interviewers. If you need notes, you could position the key bullet points behind the screen. This will enable you to glance at your notes without having to avert your gaze from the interviewer.

3. Face-to-face interviews

An invitation to attend a face-to-face interview is likely to take place in the final stages of the selection process. In many cases, this may occur during the assessment centre stage (see next section). They may also involve multiple interviews, including one-to-one interviews or a panel interview. In most cases, interviews will involve hiring managers or a mix of Human Resource staff and hiring managers.

Competency-based assessments: The face-to-face interview is likely to be in the form of a competency-based assessment. As the name suggests, it is supposed to be a test of your competence by assessing how your skills, education and background match up to what the employer is looking for. In short, they want to find out whether you have the skills relevant for the role.

The competency skills the employer seeks will be clear from their recruitment literature available online or in their brochures. By the time you get to the interview stage, you should have a good idea about the culture and values of the organisation which determines the core competencies.

At graduate level, most competencies involve transferable skills such as effective communication, teamwork, problem-solving, and analytical skills. The interview is your opportunity to demonstrate that you are the ideal candidate by showing how your experience matches the employer's requirements.

During a competency-based interview, the recruiter will ask questions that require you to give examples from your experience. Usually, these questions will be along the following lines:

"Think of an example of how you demonstrated..."

"Tell me a time when you showed..."

The interviewer will be seeking good practical examples of the key competencies from your background (i.e., work experience, involvement in co-curricular activity, volunteering, or involvement in clubs/societies at university).

The STAR technique: The STAR model is a useful technique to help you excel in competency-based interviews, by helping you to articulate yourself concisely. "STAR" is an acronym for Situation, Task, Action and Result. Use this technique to structure your answers to the interviewer's questions as outlined below:

- Situation – Briefly describe the scenario to provide context (i.e., when did it happen, who was involved, and where were you.) For instance, when I was the treasurer for the Young Entrepreneurs' Association, we completed a community project where we renovated a local playground.

- Task - Summarise the task and what you intended to achieve. For example, we wanted to repair the dilapidated playground and make it an enjoyable space for children in the community.

- Action – Describe what you actually did, with emphasis on your role (rather than the team). For example, I took the initiative to organise the team, acquire the tools and materials we used for the day, etc.

- Result – State what you achieved and any important lessons you gained from the experience. For example, the project was very successful and the playground is a popular community spot. It taught me the value of community engagement and how to work effectively as a team.

The key to performing well in competency-based interviews is preparation. The competencies that the employer will assess at interview will be broadly similar to the competencies indicated in their recruitment literature and your application form.

Therefore, there is an element of predictability you can anticipate. In the lead-up to your interview, outline good examples from your experience using the STAR technique. Practice how you will talk about these examples, matching them to the key competencies of the employer. Practice by yourself and also have mock interviews with friends. Here are some sample competency-based questions you can use:

- Describe a time when you dealt with a difficult situation.

- Give me an example of when you worked effectively in a team.

- Tell me about a situation when you had to persuade others.

- Describe a time where you were able to solve a problem creatively.

- Tell me about a time you made a decision that did not turn out for the best.

- Describe your greatest achievement.

- Give me an example of a time when you had to prioritise projects.

- Describe situations where you displayed leadership skills.

In addition to competency-based questions, you are likely to be asked about your career motivations. You should expect your knowledge of the industry and organisation to be tested. Common questions could include the following:

- Why do you want a career with this organisation?

- Where do you see yourself in five years?

- Why do you think you can have a successful career in this company?

- Why are you interested in this industry?

- What are the key challenges facing our organisation?

- What do you know about our competitors?

- What makes you interested in a career with our organisation?

Interviews are also your opportunity to find out whether the organisation is right for you. So go prepared with some questions. Good questions can also impress interviewers, particularly if they are thoughtful questions. You could consider the following questions:

- How are graduates supported during the first few years in the company?

- Describe the career progression opportunities available for graduates.

- What training and development opportunities are available for graduates?

Top tips regarding face-to-face interviews

- **Prepare your STAR examples:** Identify the key competencies for the organisation. For each competency, prepare the examples you will talk about using the STAR technique.

- **Practice, practice, practice:** Practice your examples by yourself and also ask a friend to conduct a mock interview. The more you practice, the better your interviewing technique becomes.

- **Review your application and CV:** Questions about your background and information you provided in your application are likely to come up. You will need to be ready to explain any questions posed about your application.

- **Relax the night before:** Get a good night's rest before the interview; it will help you perform at your best.

- **Getting to the venue:** Plan ahead and allow for plenty of time to get to the interview venue. Factor in how long it takes to travel and choose the most appropriate transport option. You may want to find your venue early so that you can locate a nearby café where you can relax and review your notes one final time.

- **Dress appropriately:** You should be dressed appropriately and look professional. Dressing well will help increase your confidence, too.

- **Positive body language:** Remember, body language accounts for 55% of your communication so you need to ensure that it is positive. Remember to smile, maintain your composure and keep gesticulation under control.

- **Don't lie:** Recruiters will spot inconsistencies and exaggerations in your story.

Assessment centres

Assessment centres are usually the last stage in the selection process for most medium and large employers. An assessment centre is a mixture of activities designed to test a candidate's ability and suitability for a role. The variety of tasks allows candidates to show a wider range of skills and it helps recruiters assess how candidates work with others.

Assessment centres can last from half a day to two days. They are usually held at the employer's premises, separate training facility or hotels. Candidates will take part in individual tasks and group exercises that could feature a combination of any of the following: psychometric tests, case studies (which include group discussions and presentations), e-tray exercises, competency-based interviews and social events.

The assessors on the day will typically be a mix of hiring managers and Human Resource staff. They will assess candidates' performances against their key competency frameworks. They will evaluate and determine how candidates have performed before making final decisions.

The assessors will evaluate how you match up to their job competencies and ensure that you are the right fit for their organisation. The advantage for candidates is that assessment centres provide an overall evaluation of your skills, which is likely to be fairer (e.g. under performance in one task could be compensated for in other tasks).

Assessors will be evaluating you against a range of transferable skills, e.g. commercial awareness, decision-making, analytical thinking, organisation, planning, problem solving, adaptability, and leadership.

You can expect assessment centres to include the activities outlined below:

1. **Psychometric tests** – These can involve aptitude or personality tests. Usually, aptitude tests will involve tests of your ability, e.g.

numeracy, writing, or inductive reasoning. The focus and intensity of aptitude tests can vary depending on the roles being recruited for. Technical roles (e.g. engineering) may have more of a focus on inductive reasoning and numeracy.

Personality tests usually seek to assess your personality attributes, including motivation and your preferred working styles. The objective is to understand how you will fit in with the culture of the organisation and the roles you could be best suited for. There is no right or wrong answers. You should just be yourself and answer as truthfully as you can.

2. **Case studies** – Case study exercises can be adapted for individual or group situations. They involve work-related scenarios where candidates are asked to analyse data provided and come up with solutions. The task will often ask candidates to prepare a presentation to assessors showing why they decided to take a particular course of action.

    Sometimes assessors may provide additional information midway through your task to see how you cope with unexpected developments. These exercises are usually timed, which makes it somewhat stressful. This is deliberate because assessors want to see how you behave under pressure.

3. **E-tray exercises** – These are simulations of work scenarios to assess how you deal with situations that place demands on your time, urgent tasks and information overload. Usually, you will be given a computer and be asked to respond to emails that include various requests, briefings and information that you will have to prioritise. You may also be asked to draft a report to assess your business writing ability.

    To succeed with the E-tray exercises, you need to be good at managing your time and prioritising appropriately. Ensure that you don't get lost in irrelevant detail or so overloaded with information that you lose sight of what is really urgent or important.

4. **Competency-based interviews** – These may feature during the assessment centre rather than requiring applicants to attend a separate interview. It will all depend on employers' individual recruitment practices. Large employers tend to incorporate their competency-based interviews during the assessment centre. For more information on competency-based interviews, please refer to previous section on "Interviews."

5. **Social and informal sessions** – At various points during the day, there may be informal sessions which may involve presentations, lunch, or drinks with employees. Although these sessions are in a casual setting, candidates will continue to be assessed. Maintain your enthusiasm and enjoy the opportunity to find out more about the firm but remain professional throughout.

 Top tips for assessment centres

- **Prepare:** Find out as much as possible about the assessment centre you have been invited to attend from the information you have been given and what is available online. This will aid your preparation and help you to focus on the tasks likely to come up on the day.

- **Remember you are constantly being assessed:** Everyone you meet on the day is likely to be assessing you, so do not let your guard down even during the informal sessions. Maintain a polite and friendly manner with everyone you meet.

- **Active participation:** Ensure you join in every exercise, showing that you are enthusiastic and a good team player. You don't have to be the most talkative but make sure you express your thoughts. If you see that some members of your group have been excluded from the discussion, draw them in and be the one who ensures everyone has the opportunity to contribute.

- **If you make mistakes:** Do not dwell on any mistakes you might make. Instead, focus on performing well in the next task. The mistakes you think you have made might not even be noticed by assessors.

Useful information and resources

- Resources for different assessment centre tasks: *https://www.assessmentday.co.uk/*

- Resources for psychometric tests: *https://www.savilleassessment.com/Practice-Tests*

Final year

"The end is at last in sight, but we will all need to work to get there."
– Tesema Negash

As you go into your final year, you will probably be thinking a lot more about what you will do after graduation. You should be in a more advantageous position to your peers if you have been taking all the recommended actions in the previous sections.

Do not panic if you haven't yet started taking any action to prepare for life after university. Although you will have missed certain opportunities, you can still utilise your final year to prepare for your future career. For starters, I recommend that you take the following actions:

- Schedule an appointment with a Careers Adviser at your university Careers Service. You will want to use this appointment to discuss your career intentions after graduation, have your CV reviewed and find out about any work experience opportunities available in your final year.

- Prepare an up-to-date CV which you can use when you meet the Careers Adviser.

Early deadlines on graduate schemes

The timeline in the lead-up to graduation can be very tight, considering the applications you may need to make as you also complete your academic studies. As you can see from the illustration below, your applications for graduate schemes start almost as soon as your term starts (figure 4).

Figure 4: the graduate scheme timeline

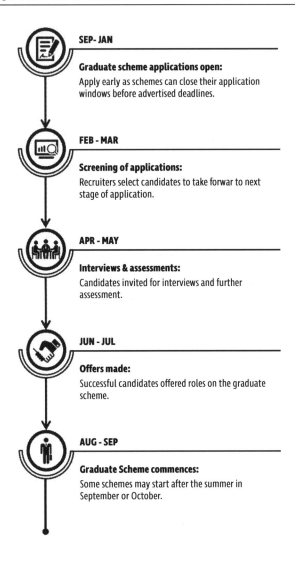

SEP- JAN

Graduate scheme applications open:
Apply early as schemes can close their application windows before advertised deadlines.

FEB - MAR

Screening of applications:
Recruiters select candidates to take forwar to next stage of application.

APR - MAY

Interviews & assessments:
Candidates invited for interviews and further assessment.

JUN - JUL

Offers made:
Successful candidates offered roles on the graduate scheme.

AUG - SEP

Graduate Scheme commences:
Some schemes may start after the summer in September or October.

It is important to note that many organisations will operate on a first-come/first-serve basis so they can close the application window as soon as they have received enough applications. Since it is not possible to determine when the application window will close, it is recommended that you apply as early as possible.

Certain vocations, such as law and teaching, have early deadlines as indicated below:

 Deadlines to watch out for

1. **Law**

   If you are interested in becoming a barrister, you need to note the following key deadlines during your final year:

   • September – Take the Bar Course Aptitude Test (BCAT).

   • November – Apply for Bar Professional Training Course (BPTC) Scholarship from the Inns of Court.

   • December – Apply for BPTC through the Bar Student Application Service (BARSAS).

   • January/February – Apply for pupillage through the Pupillage Gateway by February deadline.

   • May – Apply for membership to an Inn of Court by 31 May.

   For additional information, visit the Bar Council website: *www.barcouncil.org.uk/careers.*

2. **Postgraduate study**

If you have decided to pursue a postgraduate course immediately after you complete your undergraduate degree, you need to ensure that you do not miss the early deadlines. Although some courses will have deadlines throughout the year, many are likely to have specific deadlines that start in the autumn term. It is common, especially for popular courses, that the application window will be closed as soon as enough applications have been received. It is recommended that you are quick off the mark and apply as soon as possible to avoid disappointment.

For additional information, you can visit Prospects: *https://www.prospects.ac.uk/postgraduate-study*.

3. **Teaching**

One of the pathways for a career in teaching is through undertaking the postgraduate teacher training. In England and Wales, applications are administered through UCAS Teacher Training (UTT). The application process starts around September, so you will need to start working on your application before you start your final year.

For additional information, visit:

- UCAS Teacher Training: *https://www.ucas.com/teaching-in-the-uk*.

- The UK Department of Education website ("Get into Teaching"), which has plenty of information about a career in teaching: *https://getintoteaching.education.gov.uk/*. It includes specific advice non UK/EU nationals who may be interested in a teaching career in the UK: *https://getintoteaching.education.gov.uk/explore-my-options/overseas-applicants*.

Pursuing work experience

The final year will be very demanding so carefully consider whether you need to pursue work experience opportunities. If you have completed a vacation scheme or have an internship already lined up; then you probably need not apply for more opportunities. You can instead focus your efforts on your studies, graduate scheme applications and enjoying the last year of your student experience.

If you have not gained any work experience, then you could still apply for internships and vacation schemes. However, your options should be limited as your main focus should be applying for graduate schemes.

It is recommended that you should be very selective and target a few internship opportunities (preferably ones aimed at final year students). Prioritise the Christmas and Easter schemes so you can shift your focus to applying for graduate schemes in the summer.

Part-time work

Similar considerations will apply for part-time study in your final year as did for your penultimate year. Part-time employment may be less of a priority, depending on your financial situation and how much work experience you have. Your final year priorities will be to complete your academic study and focus on your graduate career options.

However, if you haven't got any work experience on your CV, then a part-time job may be beneficial. It may also be a necessity, if you need the job for financial reasons.

Appointments with the Careers Service

Continue meeting with your Careers Advisor and discuss your progress in searching for roles and any applications that are in the pipeline. Discuss any feedback you have received from applications that may not have been successful, so that you can improve your future performance. Enquire about upcoming recruitment events so you can plan ahead. Request for your applications to be reviewed before you submit them. Ask for any applications.

Personal tutors

Keep your personal tutor updated with your progress, academically as well as with your career search. Personal tutors can be a source of encouragement, as you face all the challenges involved in job hunting. They may help you realise options and alternatives you may not have considered.

If your tutors are also referees on your applications, remember to keep them updated about the progress of your application and interviews. You would not want them to be taken by surprise when recruiters contact them for references.

Entrepreneurship opportunities

Ideally, your early involvement in entrepreneurship activities will have enabled you to identify opportunities to start your own business. If you are determined to start your own business, you should ensure that you:

- Finalise your business plan – If you are serious about launching your venture, undertake an assessment of your market and draw up a business plan. If there is an entrepreneurship unit, request for your business plan to be reviewed. After it is reviewed, make necessary amendments.

- Business funding – Find out whether there are university grants or entrepreneurial loans that you could access. You can also research options for funding outside the university.

- Apply for support from the university incubation centre – Find out how you can apply to get support from the university incubation centre. The university's incubation centre may help you further develop and test your business ideas.

- Pitching to investors – Do some research about events where you could pitch your business idea to potential investors. For instance, find out whether there are any university events you could enrol in. You should not be limited to activities organised by your university but also consider external events, business competitions, etc.

- Business mentors – Enquire whether there are any university-affiliated business mentors or Entrepreneurs in Residence who can support you to develop your business.

Finish strong

From an academic perspective, your final year will feel extremely demanding with more reading than you think you can manage; numerous papers to submit; and final exams. With graduation in sight, you can be motivated that all the studying will soon be over and your hard work will be rewarded. Therefore it is worth knuckling down so you can achieve the best results possible.

Your overall degree results are important for your graduate job applications. Remember that graduate schemes will specify the achievement of certain grades in order to apply for certain positions.

Don't worry if your marks from first year or penultimate year were not great. You can still utilise your final year to improve your marks and your overall degree classification. On many courses, final year modules may even weigh more towards the overall degree classification. Here are a few practical tips to help you with final year studies:

- <u>Develop a consistent study pattern</u> – It is common for students resort to intense study periods (burning the candle at both ends) to get through assignments and prepare for exams. However, this approach can add to the stress and have a negative impact on your health. A less stressful approach would be to adopt a steady pattern of study throughout the term. You will be more productive and less stressed if you maintain good and regular habits throughout the term.

- <u>Plan ahead</u> - The academic year will pass very quickly and you may find yourself wishing you had more time. If you have the access to the reading lists for your modules, you could make a head start before the term begins. You could even start researching topics or assignments that you will have to do during the term. Doing this work early on will make life easier for you later in the term.

- <u>Study buddies</u> – You will not be the only one feeling the pressure of the final year, many of your colleagues will be in the same boat. If you have a close group of friends, you could collaborate more by having group study sessions which can make dull revision sessions more interesting and productive. You could motivate and encourage each other to keep morale high.

- <u>Look after your health</u> – If there was ever a time when you need to stay in tip top health, it would be your final year. Ensure that you are getting regular exercise, eating a balanced diet (which you can supplement with multivitamins) and enough sleep.

- <u>Stay positive</u> – You may feel slightly anxious during your final year, which is quite normal. However, if it feels overwhelming speak to someone like a friend or family member. Your university will have counsellors who look after student welfare and should be able to help you deal with stress. External sources of advice and help are available as referenced below:

Useful information and resources

- **Elefriends** is a safe place to listen, share and be heard:
  https://www.elefriends.org.uk/

- If you are feeling depressed, **Students against Depression** is
  a website by students for students. It offers advice, guidance
  and resources suited to the experiences of students:
  https://www.studentsagainstdepression.org/

- **Student Minds' Guide:** The guide aims to support students
  and provides useful tips on mental health:
  *https://www.mind.org.uk/information-support/tips-for-
  everyday-living/student-life/#.W_r1-OKYRqM*

Graduate success story: Ajay (India)

 Ajay K (India)

Ajay came to study in the UK as an overseas student from India. After he completed his studies in business and administration at Cranfield University, he joined the Amazon UK graduate program. He has since developed a successful career in operations management. He draws on his experience as an international student to share insights and tips for current and prospective students.

1. Why did you decide to study in the UK?

The main reason I chose to study in UK was because of the international work atmosphere that the UK provides. Studying with a class full of students brings a whole new perspective to discussions and enriches the learning experience.

2. What factors influenced your choice of university?

Prior to making my application, I did my basic research by speaking with alumni and checking the basic rankings and link to employers. Also, the availability of financial support in the form of a bursary helped to sway my decision.

3. What influenced your decision to choose the course you took?

I chose my course as I felt that it would boost my career prospects and help me make a geographical and career change.

4. Did your university experience match your expectations?

I had a really good experience in my university, including the student mix, professors, leadership development and extracurricular activities.

5. Describe your job hunting experience in the UK.

My job hunting experience was very difficult, especially as I also graduated just after the Brexit referendum. The reputation of the university was helpful in terms of opening doors to the companies where the alumni were based. In hindsight, I would have been more proactive earlier during my course, rather than waiting too late to start job hunting.

6. What advice do you have for students to help them maximise their university experience?

I would recommend students be more proactive in terms of connecting with the alumni and other professionals. Also, enjoy your university experience; it can be life changing. Step out of the comfort zone and be open-minded.

PART THREE

Graduation and transitioning into your career

CHAPTER 8

Celebrate your success

"The more you praise and celebrate your life, the more there is in life to celebrate."
– Oprah Winfrey

"Celebrate what you have accomplished, but raise the bar a little higher each time you succeed."
- Mia Hamm

Graduating from university is a significant achievement, and you should be immensely proud of yourself. The university experience is quite challenging, especially if you are an overseas student.

The journey that you have been on from the time you joined as a fresher right up to graduation may have been tougher than you had expected.

Some of the significant challenges include culture shock and having to adapt quickly to a new country, managing your academic commitments, developing your employability, and staying on top of all your other personal responsibilities.

As you look back to your university experience, I am sure you can think of many more obstacles and interesting stories about your remarkable journey.

Many students start out university thinking that they have a long time before they finish their studies. By the time graduation comes around, you are likely to feel shocked at how quickly time has flown by.

As you reminisce on your time at university, you might feel a bit nostalgic. You can be forgiven for feeling envious of new first year students, knowing how much fun they have ahead of them. Other graduates will be simply glad that their student days are over so that they can embrace a new and exciting phase of their lives.

Despite all the individual trials and challenges you have faced, you have overcome them all, and can say to yourself: "I did it!" Your graduation is definitely something to be proud of.

CHAPTER 9

Resilience for the post-graduation slump

"Nothing in the world can take the place of persistence. Talent will not; nothing is more common than unsuccessful men with talent. Genius will not; unrewarded genius is almost a proverb. Education alone will not; the world is full of educated derelicts. Persistence and determination alone are omnipotent."
– Calvin Coolidge

"Do not judge me by my success, judge me by how many times I fell down and got back up again."
– Nelson Mandela

The period after graduation can also be a time when you start to worry about your future – particularly if you have not secured a graduate role and have no concrete plans for the near future. This feeling can be compounded as you hear that some of your friends already have jobs or internships lined up after they return from their summer holidays.

In this section, I will cover one of the most difficult phases that many graduates face. It can affect graduates regardless of whether they are from the UK, EU or non-EU. I refer to it as the post-graduation slump, that period after graduation when graduates are trying to transition into careers but feel stuck in either unemployment or underemployment.

This period can last anywhere from three to eighteen months, in some cases even longer. For most of their lives, students have the security and certainty from a well-structured routine that revolves around education. After graduation, that certainty disappears. Those who have not secured graduate jobs or further study opportunities start to feel as though they have been cast adrift. Graduates find themselves wondering why they went to university and attained a qualification that no one seems to value. Social media becomes irritating as they compare themselves to peers whose careers seem to be taking off. They end up feeling like failures and ponder where they went wrong.

Although the post-graduate slump affects many graduates, it is a subject that is largely overlooked by existing literature on careers guidance. I have been through this phase and I know many other graduates who had similar experiences. It was without a doubt, one of the most trying, frustrating and challenging periods of my life.

Initially, you may not be too worried as you are still optimistic, basking in the glow of your accomplishment as a new graduate. After a few months, you can feel discouraged when nothing materialises from all the application forms and CVs you have sent out. You may even have made it to the last interview, only to receive a phone call confirming that you have not been successful.

Weeks then feel like months and months feel like forever. You may then start feeling low and discouraged, thinking that university was a colossal waste of time and money.

If you feel this way, just remember that you are not alone in this. Many other graduates have gone through this phase and eventually become successful. There is no reason why you won't achieve your breakthrough, too.

You have the rest of your life to build your career. So, it is not the end of the world if you do not secure a graduate role right away. Let us look at the actions you could take to get through this difficult phase and help you not to become disillusioned.

1. **Time to reflect and plan:** This phase could be advantageous, allowing you to reflect on your life and decide what you really want to do next. University can be so busy that you may have only had time to focus on your academic studies. With no assignment deadlines and more time to yourself, you can switch your focus to planning for your future career.

2. **Reconnect with family and friends:** Time away at university is likely to have created some distance in your relationships. In fact, some international students do not always go back home for the holidays. This phase before you find a career can be ideal for reconnecting with family and friends. Your family will be excited to have more time with you. You may resent moving back with your parents, but it has its advantages, e.g. saving on expenses, delicious home cooked meals (instead of cafeteria food) and everything else you missed during your student days.

3. **Embrace the freedom:** You may never have this freedom again, so why not use it to do the things you have always wanted to do? After your career starts, it is unlikely that you will get this opportunity again. Perhaps you have always wanted to travel a bit more, pick up a new sport or hobby or learn a language? The opportunities are endless, and they do not have to be expensive if you are resourceful.

4. **Avoid comparing yourself to others:** During this phase, it is very easy to slip into the habit of comparing yourself to peers and friends from university. You can find yourself thinking everyone else seems to be faring better based on their social media postings, jobs they have or cities they live in. Even worse, you may think others are judging you to be a failure based on others. Remember

that not everyone has to be on the same timeline. You do not all have to find graduate careers at the same time. Your time will come, and when it does it will be the right role at the right time.

It may be a good time to limit your social media usage if you find yourself drawn into the comparison game. Social media displays filtered views rather than the entirety of people's lives. Take time off social media and focus on the real relationships around you.

5. **Exercise and healthy eating:** Look after your body in times like this. It will definitely help you to beat the blues and help you stay in a positive and happy mood. Avoid the temptation of falling into a pattern of bingeing, neglecting your hygiene, sleeping too little and sleeping too much.

6. **Stay motivated:** Do not give up on your search for graduate opportunities. Continue to stay up-to-date with industry and business trends by reading and researching widely. Widen your search to include recruitment agencies as well as applying directly to employers.

7. **Talk to friends:** Remember, you are not alone in what you are experiencing. There are others out there who are going through it, or have gone through it. Find a friend from university who is going through the same experience and encourage one another. Perhaps you can find alumni who have been through similar situations, who can act as your cheerleader, encouraging you to stay on track and not give up. Understandably, you may not want to be around people and be tempted to keep to yourself. Whatever you do, do not let yourself become isolated; it will only have negative and harmful effects on you.

8. **Have a change of scenery:** Staying in the same environment when you are searching for graduate roles can get rather dreary. Opt for a change of scenery where you can work on your applications

(e.g. the local library or a café). A change of location and your usual routine will boost your mood and help you to see things differently.

9. **Increase the positive influences around you:** Stay in the company of people who inspire and encourage you. Equally, you should avoid naysayers and people whose company just seems to depress you. Read interesting books, watch inspiring movies, and listen to podcasts or TED talks by interesting and successful people.

10. **Find a mentor:** Mentoring is a relationship between two people with the objective of personal or professional development. In this relationship, the "mentor" is usually an experienced professional who is willing to share his or her experience, knowledge and guidance with a less experienced person (the "mentee"). A mentor will use his or her professional experience to support you as a mentee by offering recommendations that will assist you to improve your skills and further your career.

A mentor can help you refine your career development strategy and even assist with finding useful professional contacts. Use your personal network (family and friends) to identify a professional who may be willing to help. The set-up for mentoring can be informal, e.g. meeting up once a month over a coffee to discuss your career goals and strategies. There are also a few organisations that can help you find mentors (see below for helpful resources).

11. **Volunteer:** Find charities or community organisations that you can volunteer with. This will help you gain valuable skills and experience for your CV. Volunteering projects often involve corporate organisations which could help you to network with potential employers. You are also likely to enjoy the experience, make new friends and continue to build your network.

12. **Remember your accomplishments:** Think about everything that you have accomplished to date and what you are proud of.

This should also include positive feedback from teachers, peers, tutors, family, etc. Write them down and use this list as a point of reflection when you start feeling low.

13. **University support:** Many universities allow graduates access to careers services and other resources for a period of time after graduation. Continue to utilise these sources. Speak regularly to your careers adviser and have them look over your applications or prepare you for interviews. Also keep your personal tutor updated with your progress after graduation.

14. **Practice mindfulness:** Mindfulness is the psychological process of bringing one's focus and attention to experiences taking place in the present moment. During stressful or busy times, it is easy to stop noticing the world around us and go into "auto-pilot" mode. We can become detached and get caught up in our thoughts without stopping to realise how those thoughts are driving how we feel and behave.

During stressful times, it is easy for negative thought patterns to become reinforcing. For instance, constant rejections from job applications make you think you are unlucky or the "world is against you." These thoughts then start to sap your enthusiasm for subsequent applications or interviews. If you are not aware of these thought patterns, they can have a negative impact on your performance and overall mental health.

Practicing mindfulness can improve your focus, mental wellbeing and help you deal with anxiety and stress. Mindfulness techniques do not require prior learning and are quite easy to incorporate into your routine. Refer to links below for mindfulness resources you could use.

15. **Plan fun events in your calendar:** Having something fun in your calendar keeps you excited about the future rather than wallowing

in the slump. It does not have to be an expensive event or activity. Simply having something to look forward to in the days ahead (e.g. going to the cinema, a day at the beach) will keep you excited about the days ahead.

16. **Develop resilience:** Be patient and remember that this phase is not permanent. Eventually it will come to an end. Think of this phase as the opportunity for you to develop resilience. Resilience can be described as the ability people have to successfully overcome stressful experiences. It is that ability to bounce back or pick ourselves up when we experience adversity in our lives.

As the philosopher Nietzsche said, whatever does not kill you will make you stronger. All the techniques that you apply to stay positive and not give up during this phase will make you more resilient. Developing your resilience will help you throughout your life and make you more adaptable to dealing with adverse events. One day, you may even look back and appreciate how this experience helped you grow and shape your perspective on life.

It can feel like your life has hit rock-bottom when you are going through the post-graduation slump. You will have to overcome many of the challenges that come during this phase, such as:

- not giving up the search for a graduate role when you are getting lots of rejections,

- taking on unpaid internships or voluntary roles to gain work experience,

- living at home with your parents or relatives because you cannot afford to live on your own,

- accepting temporary or unskilled jobs to help pay the bills, etc.

Having been through it all myself, I can assure you that this phase does have an end date. It will probably occur when you least expect it. You have come a long way and accomplished a lot to get to where you are. So do not give up, keep applying the techniques outlined above and eventually you will achieve the breakthrough you need to launch your career.

 Useful information and resources

1. **TED Talks:** TED Talks are influential videos from expert speakers on a range of subjects:
   https://www.ted.com/

   Here are a few recommended inspiring videos:

   • **The surprising science of happiness (Dan Gilbert):** Dan shares about how we can all synthesize happiness:
   https://www.ted.com/talks/dan_gilbert_asks_why_are_we_happy

   • **Nature. Beauty. Gratitude (Louie Schwartzberg):** Louie's stunning video, accompanied with wise words of a Benedictine monk, is very uplifting. It will help you feel grateful for every day:
   https://www.ted.com/talks/louie_schwartzberg_nature_beauty_gratitude?language=en

   • **Living beyond limits (Amy Purdy):** When Amy was 19, she lost both her legs below the knee but now she is a pro snowboarder. Watch her talk on how to draw inspiration from life's challenges:
   https://www.ted.com/talks/amy_purdy_living_beyond_limits?language=en

- **The 3 A's of Awesome (Neil Pasricha):** Neil shares 3 secrets to leading an awesome life: *https://www.ted.com/talks/neil_pasricha_the_3_a_s_of_awesome?language=en#t-10847*

2. **Employability and Mentoring**

   - Uprising Fastlaners is an employability programme designed to help young people find careers through a series of networking, mentoring and skills workshops: *https://uprising.org.uk/programmes/fastlaners*

3. **Volunteering opportunities**

   - **Do-it.org** is a UK volunteering database which makes it easy to find opportunities to volunteer in your community: *http://doittrust.org/*

   - **TimeBank** is a charity that recruits and trains volunteers to deliver mentoring projects: *http://timebank.org.uk/*

   - **vinspired** is a volunteering charity for 14 - 25 year olds: *https://vinspired.com/*

4. **Mindfulness resources**

   - NHS information on mindfulness: *https://www.nhs.uk/conditions/stress-anxiety-depression/mindfulness/*

   - Free guided mindful exercises to practice: *http://www.freemindfulness.org/download*

5. **Uplifting music:** Music has the power to give you an almost immediate emotional hit. Whatever your tastes and

preferences, find music that has an uplifting impact on your mood to help you get through those difficult moments. Here are a few recommendations to get you started:

- "Don't Worry be Happy" (Bobby McFerrin): *https://www.youtube.com/watch?v=d-diB65scQU*

- "Happy" (Farrell Williams): *https://www.youtube.com/watch?v=ZbZSe6N_BXs*

- "Everybody's free to wear sunscreen" (Baz Luhrmann): *https://www.youtube.com/watch?v=sTJ7AzBIJoI*

6. **Adjusting to life after university:**

- *HelloGrads* offers advice and guidance to help students transition between university and real life: *https://hellograds.com/who-we-are/*

Entrepreneurship success story: Building a software business in the UK

 Vinay Nagaraju (India)

Vinay is a successful entrepreneur based in the UK. After completing his studies in Business and Administration at Cranfield University, in 2016, Vinay co-founded a privacy management software company in the UK called Data Solver, where he is currently Chief Information Officer. He shares his experience and provides useful advice for students with entrepreneurial ambitions.

1. **What was your motivation for entrepreneurship instead of being employed?**

    Start-ups have always fascinated me. There is an inherent energy and motivation to bring an idea into fruition. There is an opportunity to delve into different areas of the business such as marketing, product development, sales, funding, etc.

    More importantly, it is a wonderful opportunity to create a team and develop the vision which you start a business with.

2. **What key factors would you advise students who are interested in becoming entrepreneurs to consider when they are choosing a UK university?**

    I would suggest that prospective students do their research on the alumni profile, the university's record about entrepreneurship, and statistics about number of businesses coming out per year.

    More importantly, I would look at the university's framework for supporting entrepreneurship. If there is a dedicated entrepreneurship department, with ongoing projects and internships – there is a stronger likelihood for a better focus on entrepreneurship. I would also look at the modules of the subjects offered and find out about entrepreneurship-specific courses.

3. **If you had the chance to do it all again, what would you do differently?**

I think I would start working on the business sooner. Although we did start our business planning in time, with hindsight, we realised that we could have achieved greater progress if we had made use of the facilities much earlier. Once you complete a course, frequency of interaction with the academic circle reduces.

To make the most of your course for entrepreneurship, it will be great if you enter the course with a business idea in mind. My course was very helpful to put this business idea into perspective of a business plan, identify routes to market, funding opportunities, etc. It gave me an opportunity to look at the idea as a business before we could delve into the actual process of working through the business.

I would also talk about the business idea from day one and make sure my network knows about the business idea. There is a huge amount of support in the university community and they can be of immense help in challenging the idea further to fine tune it into a marketable product. It also provides an opportunity to look at the business idea in a critical manner and develop better strategies around your approach.

4. **What are the highlights and challenges that you can share about starting your own business?**

The key highlights about the business venture have been in securing our funding and capital, securing our first customer, developing the first cut of our product, winning a few grants, and creating the team. The highlights also include some fantastic accolades from the UK government (Department of International Trade), being part of trade missions, recognition from industry bodies such as Digital Catapult and Innovate UK.

Any start-up comes with its own challenges, including securing funding, developing product from an idea, gathering momentum from investors and customers, and team development. The key is, of course, making sure that you have the right set of people around you to seek timely advice from. And being in an entrepreneurial network such as incubators will be hugely helpful.

5. **What pearls of wisdom do you have for budding entrepreneurs whilst they are at university? In particular, how would you advise them about maximising their university experience so that they can launch entrepreneurship ventures?**

- Make sure you are a part of the start-up programs in the university. Participate in as many programs or venture competitions that you can.

- Use every opportunity you can to network – you never know who will be your mentor/business partner/ advisor/investor/guide. There is a lot of value you can gain by speaking about your idea.

- Make use of every opportunity to pitch your business idea. Show progress in developing the idea from one pitch to another. Although the audience is different, you will still be around a network of influencers and advisors who like to see progress.

- Curate advice received from people around you and incorporate that into your business pitch/plan as appropriate.

- Write your business plan. A lot of your business ideas/ thoughts formulate as you put them on paper. It will give you an opportunity to think through your product and answer key questions about the venture.

- Utilise opportunities to work on projects relating to your business idea. This can be through the university internship programme or selecting your modules/electives.

You can find more information on Vinay and his company at: *https://www.datasolver.com.*

Last thoughts

"The future belongs to those who believe in the beauty of their dreams."
– Eleanor Roosevelt

"The future belongs to those who prepare for it today."
– Malcolm X

The transition from school to university to launching a professional career can be one of the most exciting and daunting phases of our lives. As an international student, that journey is even more adventurous, given all the challenges of adapting to a new country. I hope that this book has been a useful guide to you on that journey.

As you look behind you to see just how far you have come, take in the view just for a moment. Recall all the obstacles and challenges that you faced. There were tough times, I am sure, but you survived and made it this far.

As you look ahead to your future, remember your accomplishments and let that propel you as you launch your career. It is your time to flourish and to pursue your dream more passionately than ever.

Share your story

I would love to hear about your experience as an international student. Please share your story by emailing me at: *marvin@internationalstudentpathfinder.com*.

You can also visit the website *www.internationalstudentpathfinder.com* to find more resources, information and updates.

What did you think of *International Student Pathfinder?*

Firstly, thank you for purchasing this book. I know you could have picked any number of books, but you picked this book and for that I am extremely grateful!

I hope that you enjoyed it and found it beneficial. I would be grateful if you could take some time to post a review on Amazon. Your feedback and support will help me to improve my writing craft and develop better solutions for students in future projects.

Feel free to share this book with your friends and family by posting to Facebook and Twitter.

I wish you all the best in your future!

Appendices

Appendix 1: Additional sources of information on university related topics

1. **General information for international students**

   - British Council - *https://study-uk.britishcouncil.org/*

   - UK Council for International Student Affairs (UKCISA) - *https://www.ukcisa.org.uk/*

2. **Searching and applying for courses**

   - Universities and Colleges Admissions Service (UCAS) - *https://www.ucas.com/*

   - Heap Online - *http://www.heaponline.co.uk/*

   - UNISTATS - *https://unistats.ac.uk/*

3. **Funding and scholarships**

   - Commonwealth Scholarships and fellowships - *http://cscuk.dfid.gov.uk/apply/*

   - Chevening Scholarships - *http://www.chevening.org/*

   - Marshall Scholarship - *http://www.marshallscholarship.org/*

   - Funding for EU students studying in Scotland - *http://www.saas.gov.uk/full_time/ug/eu/index.htm*

- Funding for EU students in Wales -
  https://www.studentfinancewales.co.uk/eu.aspx

- Funding for EU students studying in England -
  https://www.gov.uk/student-finance/eu-students

- Funding for EU students studying in N.Ireland -
  https://www.nidirect.gov.uk/articles/how-apply-finance-eu-students

- Great India Scholarships -
  https://www.britishcouncil.in/study-uk/scholarships/great-scholarships

4. Budgeting and living costs

- International student calculator -
  https://international.studentcalculator.org/

5. Visas and Immigration

- The UK Government Visas and Immigration website -
  https://www.gov.uk/government/organisations/uk-visas-and-immigration

6. Students with disabilities

- Disability Rights UK -
  https://www.disabilityrightsuk.org/

7. Books

- University Degree Course Offers by Brian Heap.

Appendix 2: The Times Top 100 Graduate Employers

Accenture	Diageo
Aecom	DLA Piper
Airbus	Dyson
Aldi	E.ON
Allen & Overy	Exxonmobil
Amazon	EY
Apple	Facebook
Army	Freshfields Bruckhaus Deringer
Arup	Frontline
AstraZeneca	GCHQ
Atkins	GE
BAE Systems	Goldman Sachs
Bain & Company	Google
Baker & Mckenzie	Grant Thornton
Bank of England	GSK
Barclays	Herbert Smith Freehills
BBC	Hogan Lovells
Bloomberg	HSBC
BMW Group	IBM
Boots	Irwin Mitchell
Boston Consulting Group	Jaguar Land Rover
BP	John Lewis Partnership
BT	JP Morgan
Cancer Research UK	KPMG
Centrica	L'Oreal
Charityworks	Lidl
Citi	Linklaters
Civil Service Fast Stream	Lloyd's
Clifford Chance	Lloyds Banking Group
CMS	Local Government
Danone	Marks & Spencer
Deloitte	Mars
Deutsche Bank	McDonald's Restaurants

McKinsey & Company	Rolls-Royce
Mi5 - The Security Service	Royal Navy
Microsoft	Santander
Morgan Stanley	Savills
Mott Macdonald	Shell
Nestlé	Siemens
Network Rail	Sky
Newton Europe	Slaughter and May
NHS	Teach First
Norton Rose Fulbright	Tesco
Oxfam	Think Ahead
Penguin Random House	UBS
Police Now	Unilever
Procter & Gamble	Virgin Media
PwC	Wellcome
RAF	White & Case
RBS	WPP

Bibliography

1. Centre for Entreprenuers. (2017). *Putting the Uni in Unicorn: The role of universities in supporting high-growth graduate start-ups.*

2. Department for Education (UK). (2017). *Teaching Excellence and Student Outcomes Framework Specification.*

3. E Department for Education (UK). (2018). *Graduate outcomes (LEO): Employment and earnings outcomes of higher education graduates by subject studied and graduate characteristics.* Department of Education.

4. HECSU/ AGCAS. (2017/18). *What do Graduates do?* Graduate Prospects Ltd .

5. High Fliers. (2018). *The Graduate Market in 2018*. High Fliers Research Ltd.

6. Quality Assurance Agency for Higher Education. (2018). *Enterprise and Entrepreneurship Education: Guidance for Higher Education Providers.*

7. The Economist. (2018). University Rankings: Higher and Higher Education . *The Economist May 19th 2018.*

8. Waltz, D. M. *Improving Student Employability.* www.jobs.ac.uk.

9. Yorke, P. M. (2006). *Employability in Higher Education: what it is - what it is not.* The Higher Education Academy.

Websites sources:

- *https://www.hecsu.ac.uk/assets/assets/documents/seven_years_ on.pdf*

- *https://www.justoncampus.co.uk/wp-content/uploads/2016-AGR-Annual-Survey-2.pdf*

- *https://www.highfliers.co.uk/download/2018/graduate_market/ GMReport18.pdf*

- *https://www.ons.gov.uk/employmentandlabourmarket/ peopleinwork/employmentandemployeetypes/articles/graduatesint heuklabourmarket/2017#main-points*

- *https://ise.org.uk/page/Graduatejobs*

Endnotes

1. *https://www.topuniversities.com/student-info/student-finance/how-much-does-it-cost-study-uk*

2. *https://www.timeshighereducation.com/sites/default/files/breaking_news_files/international_undergraduate_students_-_the_uks_competitive_advantage_report_v3.pdf*

3. Ibid

4. *https://www.ukcisa.org.uk/Research--Policy/Statistics/International-student-statistics-UK-higher-education*

5. *http://www.universitiesuk.ac.uk/facts-and-stats/Pages/impact-of-higher-education.aspx*

6. *https://www.timeshighereducation.com/sites/default/files/breaking_news_files/international_undergraduate_students_-_the_uks_competitive_advantage_report_v3.pdf*

7. Ibid

8. Ibid

9. Ibid

10. Ibid

11. The Higher Education Careers Service Unit (HECSU)/The Association of Graduate Careers Advisory Services (AGCAS)

12. *https://www.topuniversities.com/student-info/student-finance/ how-much-does-it-cost-study-uk*

13. *https://www.independent.co.uk/student/news/university-world- ranking-position-is-more-important-that-quality-of-teaching-when- it-comes-to-10418176.html*

14. (High Fliers, 2018)

15. See Appendix 2 for *The Times Top 100 Graduate Employers in the UK*. (Source: the Graduate Market in 2018)

16. *"University Rankings: Higher and higher education"*; The Economist (19th May 2018)

17. (Yorke, 2006) *http://www.employability.ed.ac.uk/documents/Staff/ HEA-Employability_in_HE(Is,IsNot).pdf*

18. Longitudinal Education Outcome (LEO), March 2018.

a MJN Publishing book
printed 2019

45399757R00133

Made in the USA
Middletown, DE
16 May 2019